PROFESSIONAL · ENHANCEMENT · SERIES

Infants & Toddlers

Join us on the Web at

EarlyChildEd.delmar.com

Infants & Toddlers

Terri Swim

DELMAR
CENGAGE Learning™

Australia • Canada • Mexico • Singapore • Spain • United Kingdom • United States

Infants & Toddlers

Terri Swim

For product information and technology assistance, contact us at
Cengage Learning Customer & Sales Support, 1-800-354-9706

For permission to use material from this text or product, submit all requests online at **cengage.com/permissions**
Further permissions questions can be emailed to

Library of Congress Control Number: 2007005386

ISBN-13: 978-1-4180-1667-8

ISBN-10: 1-4180-1667-5

Delmar Cengage Learning
5 Maxwell Drive
Clifton Park, NY 12065-2919
USA

Cengage Learning products are represented in Canada by Nelson Education, Ltd.

For your lifelong learning solutions, visit
delmar.cengage.com

Visit our corporate website at **www.cengage.com**

Notice to the Reader

Printed in Canada
3 4 5 6 7 8 9 12 11 10 09 08

TABLE OF CONTENTS

INTRODUCTION

Throughout a college preparation program to become an early childhood educator, students take many courses and read many textbooks. Their knowledge grows as they accumulate ideas from lectures, reading, experiences, and discussions. When they finish their coursework, graduate, and move into their first teaching positions, students often leave behind some of the books they have used. The hope is, however, that they take with them the important ideas from their classes and books as they begin their own professional practice.

More experienced colleagues or mentors sometimes support teachers in their first teaching positions, helping them make the transition from the college classroom to being responsible for a group of young children. Other times, new teachers are left to travel their own paths, relying on their own resources. Whatever your situation, this professional enhancement guide is designed to provide reminders of things you have learned and resources to help you make sense of and apply what you learned during your college coursework.

Teachers of young children are under great pressure today. Families demand support in their difficult tasks of child rearing in today's fast-paced and changing world. Some families become so overwhelmed with the tasks of parenting that they seem to leave too much responsibility on the shoulders of teachers and caregivers. From administrators and institutions, there are expectations that sometimes seem overwhelming. Teachers are being held accountable for children's learning in ways unprecedented in even the recent past. Public scrutiny has led to insistence on teaching practices that may seem contrary to the best interests of children or their teachers. This is even true for infant and toddler teachers. Many states have created or are creating developmental standards to guide the work of infant-toddler teachers and to hold them accountable for assessing children's progress. New teachers may find themselves caught between the realities of the schools or centers where they are working, and their own philosophies and ideals of working with children. When faced with such dilemmas, these individuals need to be able to fall back and reflect on what they know of best practices, renewing their professional determination to make appropriate decisions for children.

This book provides some tools for that reflection:

- Tips for getting started in your new environment
- Suggestions for becoming a reflective professional, including the Code of Ethical Conduct for early childhood educators
- Information about typical developmental patterns for infants and toddlers
- Key ideas about Developmentally Appropriate Practice, the process of decision making that allows teachers to provide optimally challenging environments for infants and toddlers
- Tools to assist teachers in making observations and gathering data on children to help set appropriate goals for individual children
- Guides for planning appropriate classroom experiences, sample lesson plans, and suggestions for selecting appropriate materials
- Strategies for introducing children to the joys of literacy as well as a list of quality books for infants and toddlers
- Resources, or places for accessing resources, for professional development and completing your work as an early childhood educator
- Case studies of relevant, realistic situations you may face, as well as best practices for successfully navigating through them
- Insight into current issues and trends facing early childhood educators who work with infant and toddlers

Becoming a teacher is a continuing process of growing, learning, reflecting, and discovering through experience. Having these resources will help you along your way. Good luck on your journey!

A special thanks to Nicole Hall for her endless hours in the library searching and locating quality children's literature and various teacher resources.

REFLECTIONS FOR GROWING TEACHERS

Teachers spend most of their time working with young children and their families. During the course of a day, questions and concerns arise, and decisions have to be made. Thus, it is important that teachers become reflective about their work. Too often, teachers believe they are too busy to spend time thinking. Rather, experienced professional teachers learn that reflection sustains their best work. Growing teachers need to take time on a regular basis to consider the questions and concerns that arise from their practice. Many teachers use journals to keep track of the process because their reflections are easily stored, accessed, and reviewed, just like with a portfolio of children's work.

Use some of these questions to begin your professional reflections. For example, select one or two questions a day to respond to in your professional journal. At the end of the week, review what you have written and decide what, if any, changes you need to make or professional development experiences that would benefit you. Eventually, you will not rely on this list of questions, but rather you will create questions from your own experience.

QUESTIONS FOR REFLECTION

This day would have been better if _____

_____

_____.

I think I need to know more about_____

_____

_____.

One new thing I think I will try this week is _____

_____

_____.

The highlight of this week was _____

_____

_____.

The observations this week made me think more about _____

_____

_____.

I think my favorite creative activity this year was _____

_____

_____.

One area where my teaching is changing is _____

_____

_____.

One area where my teaching needs to change is _____

_____

_____.

I just do not understand why _____

_____

_____.

I loved my job this week when _____

_____

_____.

I hated my job this week when _____

_____

_____.

One thing I can try to make that negative situation better next week is _____

_____

_____.

The funniest thing I heard a child say this week was_____

_____

_____.

The family member I feel most comfortable with is _____

_____

_____.

And I think the reason for that is _____

_____

_____.

The family member I feel least comfortable with is _____

_____

_____.

And I think the reason for that is _____

_____

_____.

The biggest gains in learning have been made by _____

_____

_____.

And I think this is because _____

_____

_____.

I am working on a bad habit of _____

_____

_____.

Has my attitude about teaching changed this year? Why or why not? _____

_____

_____.

What have I done lately to spark the children's imagination and creativity? _____

_____

_____.

One quote that I like to keep in mind is   _____

_____

_____.

Dealing with _____ is the most difficult thing I had to face recently because_____

_____

_____.

My teaching style has been most influenced by _____

_____

_____.

In thinking more about math and science in my curriculum, I believe_____

_____

_____.

If I were going to advise a brand-new teacher, the most helpful piece of advice would be _____

_____

_____.

I have been trying to facilitate friendships among the children by _____

_____

_____.

I really need to get started _____

_____

_____.

I used to _____, but now I _____
_____
_____.

The child who has helped me learn the most is _____. I learned _____
_____
_____.

I have grown in my communication by _____
_____
_____.

The best thing I have learned by observing is _____
_____
_____.

I still do not understand why _____
_____
_____.

One mistake I used to make that I do not make any longer is _____
_____
_____.

When I start the next year of teaching, one thing I will do more of is _____
_____
_____.

When I start the next year of teaching, one thing I won't do is_____
_____
_____.

One way I can help my children feel more competent is _____
_____
_____.

Something that I enjoy that I could share with the children in my class is _____

_____

_____.

When children have difficulty sharing, I _____

Adapted from ideas in Nilsen, B. A., *Week by Week: Documenting the Development of Young Children,* 3rd ed., published by Thomson Delmar Learning.

Remember that you are a role model for the children. They are constantly watching how you dress, what you say, and what you do.

BE A PROFESSIONAL

- Dress comfortably, yet conservatively, and follow your employer's clothing expectations. (You will probably be expected to wear closed-toe shoes to be safe and active with children; clothing should be clean, modest, and comfortable.)

- Be prepared and on time consistently.

- Avoid excessive absences.

- Always use appropriate language with children and adults.

- Form partnerships by being positive when talking to family members and showing that you are forming a positive relationship with their child. "Catch children doing something right" and share those accomplishments with parents/family members. Challenges with children should be discussed after you have established trust with the family.

- Become familiar with the National Association for the Education of Young Children's Code of Ethical Conduct.

BE A TEAM PLAYER

- Collaborate with team members to help you learn the parameters of your new position.

- Don't be afraid to ask questions or ask for guidance from teammates.

- Show your support of the team and be responsible.

- Step in to do your share of the work; don't expect others to clean up after you.

- Help others whenever possible.

- Respect others' ideas and avoid telling them how to do things.

- Strive to balance your ability to make decisions with following the lead of others.

LEARN ABOUT CHILDREN

- Be aware of children's development physically, socially, emotionally, and cognitively.

- Assess children's development and plan curriculum that will enhance it.

- Be aware that children will test you! (Children, especially of school age, will expect that you don't know the rules and may try to convince you to let them do things they have not been allowed to do previously.)

- Never hesitate to double-check something with your teammates when you are in doubt.

- Use positive management techniques with children.

MANAGEMENT TECHNIQUES FOR GAINING CHILDREN'S COOPERATION

Myriad techniques are useful for helping children cooperate. The following techniques are more preventive in nature. Children need respectful reminders of expectations and adult support to help them perform to those expectations. Be sure that your expectations are age appropriate and individually appropriate.

- Use positive phrases and state exactly what you expect children to do. Saying "Throw your paper towel in this trash can" while pointing is more effective than "Don't throw it on the floor."

- Avoid the words "no" and "don't." Be clear about what you want children to do, not what you don't want them to do.

- With older infants and toddlers, sequence directions using "When-then." For example, "When you put the truck on the block shelf, then we can go outside."

- Stay close. Merely standing near children can be enough to help them manage behavior. Be aware, however, that if you are talking to another adult, children may act out because they are aware that they do not have your attention.

- Offer sufficient and appropriate choices. Children need a variety of activities that interest them and that will create opportunities for success.

- Help children solve their problem rather than immediately doing it for them. Provide words for each child so that children can "talk" to one another about the problem and lay the foundation for seeing another perspective. For example, Yugi wants to play with the drum, and Conner wants to play with the drum. "You *both* want to play with the drum. How can you both use the drum?" Pause. While pointing, "Conner, can you beat the drum on this side and have Yugi beat the drum on this side?"

CODE OF ETHICAL CONDUCT

As mentioned earlier, early childhood educators must familiarize themselves with the National Association for the Education of Young Children's (NAEYC) Code of Ethical Conduct and Statement of Commitment. This document was created to assist teachers and other early childhood education professionals solve ethical dilemmas. Although the Code is not prescriptive in telling you how to behave, it provides guidelines for making decisions. Not all educational decisions that you make will require the use of the Code. For example, deciding whether the toddlers will brush their teeth immediately after eating lunch or after being read a story does not require ethical consideration. Other situations that you face will require the use of the Code. When two or more components of the Code apply and suggest different courses of action, you will need to engage in a process to decide how to resolve the dilemma.

To assist you in learning about professional ethics, the next pages contain the Code of Ethical Conduct in its entirety. After reading this document, please respond to the Case Study that follows. This section closes with a list of resources for further exploring professional ethics.

Code of Ethical Conduct and Statement of Commitment

A position statement of the National Association for the Education of Young Children

Revised April 2005

PREAMBLE

NAEYC recognizes that those who work with young children face many daily decisions that have moral and ethical implications. The NAEYC Code of Ethical Conduct offers guidelines for responsible behavior and sets forth a common basis for resolving the principal ethical dilemmas encountered in early childhood care and education. The Statement of Commitment is not part of the Code but is a personal acknowledgement of an individual's willingness to embrace the distinctive values and moral obligations of the field of early childhood care and education. The primary focus of the Code is on daily practice with children and their families in programs for children from birth through 8 years of age, such as infant/toddler programs, preschool and prekindergarten programs, child care centers, hospital and child life settings, family child care homes, kindergartens, and primary classrooms. When the issues involve young children, then these provisions also apply to specialists who do not work directly with children, including program administrators, parent educators, early childhood adult educators, and officials with responsibility for program monitoring and licensing. (Note: See also the "Code of Ethical Conduct: Supplement for Early Childhood Adult Educators.")

Core Values

Standards of ethical behavior in early childhood care and education are based on commitment to the following core values that are deeply rooted in the history of the field of early childhood care and education. We have made a commitment to:

- Appreciate childhood as a unique and valuable stage of the human life cycle

- Base our work on knowledge of how children develop and learn

- Appreciate and support the bond between the child and family

- Recognize that children are best understood and supported in the context of family, culture,* community, and society

- Respect the dignity, worth, and uniqueness of each individual (child, family member, and colleague)

- Respect diversity in children, families, and colleagues

Culture includes ethnicity, racial identity, economic level, family structure, language, and religious and political beliefs, which profoundly influence each child's development and relationship to the world.

■ Recognize that children and adults achieve their full potential in the context of relationships that are based on trust and respect

Conceptual Framework

The Code sets forth a framework of professional responsibilities in four sections. Each section addresses an area of professional relationships: (1) with children, (2) with families, (3) among colleagues, and (4) with the community and society. Each section includes an introduction to the primary responsibilities of the early childhood practitioner in that context. The introduction is followed by (1) a set of ideals that reflect exemplary professional practice and (2) a set of principles describing practices that are required, prohibited, or permitted. The ideals reflect the aspirations of practitioners. The principles guide conduct and assist practitioners in resolving ethical dilemmas.* Both ideals and principles are intended to direct practitioners to those questions which, when responsibly answered, can provide the basis for conscientious decision making. While the Code provides specific direction for addressing some ethical dilemmas, many others will require the practitioner to combine the guidance of the Code with professional judgment. The ideals and principles in this Code present a shared framework of professional responsibility that affirms our commitment to the core values of our field. The Code publicly acknowledges the responsibilities that we in the field have assumed and in so doing supports ethical behavior in our work. Practitioners who face situations with ethical dimensions are urged to seek guidance in the applicable parts of this Code and in the spirit that informs the whole. Often, "the right answer"— the best ethical course of action to take—is not obvious. There may be no readily apparent, positive way to handle a situation. When one important value contradicts another, we face an ethical dilemma. When we face a dilemma, it is our professional responsibility to consult the Code and all relevant parties to find the most ethical resolution.

SECTION I: ETHICAL RESPONSIBILITIES TO CHILDREN

Childhood is a unique and valuable stage in the human life cycle. Our paramount responsibility is to provide care and education in settings that are safe, healthy, nurturing, and responsive for each child. We are committed to supporting children's development and

---

*There is not necessarily a corresponding principle for each ideal.

learning; respecting individual differences; and helping children learn to live, play, and work cooperatively. We are also committed to promoting children's self-awareness, competence, self-worth, resiliency, and physical well-being.

Ideals

I-1.1—To be familiar with the knowledge base of early childhood care and education and to stay informed through continuing education and training.

I-1.2—To base program practices upon current knowledge and research in the field of early childhood education, child development, and related disciplines, as well as on particular knowledge of each child.

I-1.3—To recognize and respect the unique qualities, abilities, and potential of each child.

I-1.4—To appreciate the vulnerability of children and their dependence on adults.

I-1.5—To create and maintain safe and healthy settings that foster children's social, emotional, cognitive, and physical development and that respect their dignity and their contributions.

I-1.6—To use assessment instruments and strategies that are appropriate for the children to be assessed, that are used only for the purposes for which they were designed, and that have the potential to benefit children.

I-1.7—To use assessment information to understand and support children's development and learning, to support instruction, and to identify children who may need additional services.

I-1.8—To support the right of each child to play and learn in an inclusive environment that meets the needs of children with and without disabilities.

I-1.9—To advocate for and ensure that all children, including those with special needs, have access to the support services needed to be successful.

I-1.10—To ensure that each child's culture, language, ethnicity, and family structure are recognized and valued in the program.

I-1.11—To provide all children with experiences in a language that they know, as well as support children in maintaining the use of their home language and in learning English.

I-1.12—To work with families to provide a safe and smooth transition as children and families move from one program to the next.

Principles

P-1.1—Above all, we shall not harm children. We shall not participate in practices that are emotionally damaging, physically harmful, disrespectful, degrading, dangerous, exploitative, or intimidating to children. This principle has precedence over all others in this Code.

P-1.2—We shall care for and educate children in positive emotional and social environments that are cognitively stimulating and that support each child's culture, language, ethnicity, and family structure.

P-1.3—We shall not participate in practices that discriminate against children by denying benefits, giving special advantages, or excluding them from programs or activities on the basis of their sex, race, national origin, religious beliefs, medical condition, disability, or the marital status/family structure, sexual orientation, or religious beliefs or other affiliations of their families. (Aspects of this principle do not apply in programs that have a lawful mandate to provide services to a particular population of children.)

P-1.4—We shall involve all those with relevant knowledge (including families and staff) in decisions concerning a child, as appropriate, ensuring confidentiality of sensitive information.

P-1.5—We shall use appropriate assessment systems, which include multiple sources of information, to provide information on children's learning and development.

P-1.6—We shall strive to ensure that decisions such as those related to enrollment, retention, or assignment to special education services, will be based on multiple sources of information and will never be based on a single assessment, such as a test score or a single observation.

P-1.7—We shall strive to build individual relationships with each child; make individualized adaptations in teaching strategies, learning environments, and curricula; and consult with the family so that each child benefits from the program. If after such efforts have been exhausted, the current placement does not meet a child's needs, or the child is seriously jeopardizing the ability of other children to benefit from the program, we shall collaborate with the child's family and appropriate specialists to determine the additional services needed and/or the placement option(s) most likely to ensure the child's success. (Aspects of this principle may not apply in programs that have a lawful mandate to provide services to a particular population of children.)

P-1.8—We shall be familiar with the risk factors for and symptoms of child abuse and neglect, including physical, sexual, verbal, and emotional abuse and physical, emotional, educational, and medical neglect. We shall know and follow state laws and community procedures that protect children against abuse and neglect.

P-1.9—When we have reasonable cause to suspect child abuse or neglect, we shall report it to the appropriate community agency and follow up to ensure that appropriate action has been taken. When appropriate, parents or guardians will be informed that the referral will be or has been made.

P-1.10—When another person tells us of his or her suspicion that a child is being abused or neglected, we shall assist that person in taking appropriate action in order to protect the child.

P-1.11—When we become aware of a practice or situation that endangers the health, safety, or well-being of children, we have an ethical responsibility to protect children or inform parents and/or others who can.

SECTION II: ETHICAL RESPONSIBILITIES TO FAMILIES

Families* are of primary importance in children's development. Because the family and the early childhood practitioner have a common interest in the child's well-being, we acknowledge a primary responsibility to bring about communication, cooperation, and collaboration between the home and early childhood program in ways that enhance the child's development.

Ideals

I-2.1—To be familiar with the knowledge base related to working effectively with families and to stay informed through continuing education and training.

I-2.2—To develop relationships of mutual trust and create partnerships with the families we serve.

---

*The term *family* may include those adults, besides parents, with the responsibility of being involved in educating, nurturing, and advocating for the child.

I-2.3—To welcome all family members and encourage them to participate in the program.

I-2.4—To listen to families, acknowledge and build upon their strengths and competencies, and learn from families as we support them in their task of nurturing children.

I-2.5—To respect the dignity and preferences of each family and to make an effort to learn about its structure, culture, language, customs, and beliefs.

I-2.6—To acknowledge families' childrearing values and their right to make decisions for their children.

I-2.7—To share information about each child's education and development with families and to help them understand and appreciate the current knowledge base of the early childhood profession.

I-2.8—To help family members enhance their understanding of their children and support the continuing development of their skills as parents.

I-2.9—To participate in building support networks for families by providing them with opportunities to interact with program staff, other families, community resources, and professional services.

Principles

P-2.1—We shall not deny family members access to their child's classroom or program setting unless access is denied by court order or other legal restriction.

P-2.2—We shall inform families of program philosophy, policies, curriculum, assessment system, and personnel qualifications, and explain why we teach as we do—which should be in accordance with our ethical responsibilities to children (see Section I).

P-2.3—We shall inform families of and, when appropriate, involve them in policy decisions.

P-2.4—We shall involve the family in significant decisions affecting their child.

P-2.5—We shall make every effort to communicate effectively with all families in a language that they understand. We shall use community resources for translation and interpretation when we do not have sufficient resources in our own programs.

P-2.6—As families share information with us about their children and families, we shall consider this information to plan and implement the program.

P-2.7—We shall inform families about the nature and purpose of the program's child assessments and how data about their child will be used.

P-2.8—We shall treat child assessment information confidentially and share this information only when there is a legitimate need for it.

P-2.9—We shall inform the family of injuries and incidents involving their child, of risks such as exposures to communicable diseases that might result in infection, and of occurrences that might result in emotional stress.

P-2.10—Families shall be fully informed of any proposed research projects involving their children and shall have the opportunity to give or withhold consent without penalty. We shall not permit or participate in research that could in any way hinder the education, development, or well-being of children.

P-2.11—We shall not engage in or support exploitation of families. We shall not use our relationship with a family for private advantage or personal gain, or enter into relationships with family members that might impair our effectiveness working with their children.

P-2.12—We shall develop written policies for the protection of confidentiality and the disclosure of children's records. These policy documents shall be made available to all program personnel and families. Disclosure of children's records beyond family members, program personnel, and consultants having an obligation of confidentiality shall require familial consent (except in cases of abuse or neglect).

P-2.13—We shall maintain confidentiality and shall respect the family's right to privacy, refraining from disclosure of confidential information and intrusion into family life. However, when we have reason to believe that a child's welfare is at risk, it is permissible to share confidential information with agencies, as well as with individuals who have legal responsibility for intervening in the child's interest.

P-2.14—In cases where family members are in conflict with one another, we shall work openly, sharing our observations of the child, to help all parties involved make informed decisions. We shall refrain from becoming an advocate for one party.

P-2.15—We shall be familiar with and appropriately refer families to community resources and professional support services. After a referral has been made, we shall follow up to ensure that services have been appropriately provided.

SECTION III: ETHICAL RESPONSIBILITIES TO COLLEAGUES

In a caring, cooperative workplace, human dignity is respected, professional satisfaction is promoted, and positive relationships are developed and sustained. Based upon our core values, our primary responsibility to colleagues is to establish and maintain settings and relationships that support productive work and meet professional needs. The same ideals that apply to children also apply as we interact with adults in the workplace.

A—Responsibilities to Co-Workers

Ideals

I-3A.1—To establish and maintain relationships of respect, trust, confidentiality, collaboration, and cooperation with co-workers.

I-3A.2—To share resources with co-workers, collaborating to ensure that the best possible early childhood care and education program is provided.

I-3A.3—To support co-workers in meeting their professional needs and in their professional development.

I-3A.4—To accord co-workers due recognition of professional achievement.

Principles

P-3A.1—We shall recognize the contributions of colleagues to our program and not participate in practices that diminish their reputations or impair their effectiveness in working with children and families.

P-3A.2—When we have concerns about the professional behavior of a co-worker, we shall first let that person know of our concern in a way that shows respect for personal dignity and for the diversity to be found among staff members, and then attempt to resolve the matter collegially and in a confidential manner.

P-3A.3—We shall exercise care in expressing views regarding the personal attributes or professional conduct of co-workers. Statements should be based on firsthand knowledge, not hearsay, and relevant to the interests of children and programs.

P-3A.4—We shall not participate in practices that discriminate against a co-worker because of sex, race, national origin, religious beliefs or other affiliations, age, marital status/family structure, disability, or sexual orientation.

B—Responsibilities to Employers

Ideals

I-3B.1—To assist the program in providing the highest quality of service.

I-3B.2—To do nothing that diminishes the reputation of the program in which we work unless it is violating laws and regulations designed to protect children or is violating the provisions of this Code.

Principles

P-3B.1—We shall follow all program policies. When we do not agree with program policies, we shall attempt to effect change through constructive action within the organization.

P-3B.2—We shall speak or act on behalf of an organization only when authorized. We shall take care to acknowledge when we are speaking for the organization and when we are expressing a personal judgment.

P-3B.3—We shall not violate laws or regulations designed to protect children and shall take appropriate action consistent with this Code when aware of such violations.

P-3B.4—If we have concerns about a colleague's behavior, and children's well-being is not at risk, we may address the concern with that individual. If children are at risk or the situation does not improve after it has been brought to the colleague's attention, we shall report the colleague's unethical or incompetent behavior to an appropriate authority.

P-3B.5—When we have a concern about circumstances or conditions that impact the quality of care and education within the program, we shall inform the program's administration or, when necessary, other appropriate authorities.

C—Responsibilities to Employees

Ideals

I-3C.1—To promote safe and healthy working conditions and policies that foster mutual respect, cooperation, collaboration, competence, well-being, confidentiality, and self esteem in staff members.

I-3C.2—To create and maintain a climate of trust and candor that will enable staff to speak and act in the best interests of children, families, and the field of early childhood care and education.

I-3C.3—To strive to secure adequate and equitable compensation (salary and benefits) for those who work with or on behalf of young children.

I-3C.4—To encourage and support continual development of employees in becoming more skilled and knowledgeable practitioners.

Principles

P-3C.1—In decisions concerning children and programs, we shall draw upon the education, training, experience, and expertise of staff members.

P-3C.2—We shall provide staff members with safe and supportive working conditions that honor confidences and permit them to carry out their responsibilities through fair performance evaluation, written grievance procedures, constructive feedback, and opportunities for continuing professional development and advancement.

P-3C.3—We shall develop and maintain comprehensive written personnel policies that define program standards. These policies shall be given to new staff members and shall be available and easily accessible for review by all staff members.

P-3C.4—We shall inform employees whose performance does not meet program expectations of areas of concern and, when possible, assist in improving their performance.

P-3C.5—We shall conduct employee dismissals for just cause, in accordance with all applicable laws and regulations. We shall inform employees who are dismissed of the reasons for their termination. When a dismissal is for cause, justification must be based on evidence of inadequate or inappropriate behavior that is accurately documented, current, and available for the employee to review.

P-3C.6—In making evaluations and recommendations, we shall make judgments based on fact and relevant to the interests of children and programs.

P-3C.7—We shall make hiring, retention, termination, and promotion decisions based solely on a person's competence, record of accomplishment, ability to carry out the responsibilities of the position, and professional preparation specific to the developmental levels of children in his/her care.

P-3C.8—We shall not make hiring, retention, termination, and promotion decisions based on an individual's sex, race, national origin, religious beliefs or other affiliations, age, marital status/family structure, disability, or sexual orientation. We shall be familiar with and observe laws and regulations that pertain to employment discrimination. (Aspects of this principle do not apply to programs that have a lawful mandate to determine eligibility based on one or more of the criteria identified above.)

P-3C.9—We shall maintain confidentiality in dealing with issues related to an employee's job performance and shall respect an employee's right to privacy regarding personal issues.

SECTION IV: ETHICAL RESPONSIBILITIES TO COMMUNITY AND SOCIETY

Early childhood programs operate within the context of their immediate community made up of families and other institutions concerned with children's welfare. Our responsibilities to the community are to provide programs that meet the diverse needs of families, to cooperate with agencies and professions that share the responsibility for children, to assist families in gaining access to those agencies and allied professionals, and to assist in the development of community programs that are needed but not currently available. As individuals, we acknowledge our responsibility to provide the best possible programs of care and education for children and to conduct ourselves with honesty and integrity. Because of our specialized expertise in early childhood development and education and because the larger society shares responsibility for the welfare and protection of young children, we acknowledge a collective obligation to advocate for the best interests of children within early childhood programs and in the larger community and to serve as a voice for young children everywhere. The ideals and principles in this section are presented to distinguish between those that pertain to the work of the individual early childhood educator and those that more typically are engaged in collectively on behalf of the best interests of children—with the understanding that individual early childhood educators have a shared responsibility for addressing the ideals and principles that are identified as "collective."

Ideal (Individual)
I-4.1—To provide the community with high-quality early childhood care and education programs and services.

Ideals (Collective)
I-4.2—To promote cooperation among professionals and agencies and interdisciplinary collaboration among professions concerned

with addressing issues in the health, education, and well-being of young children, their families, and their early childhood educators.

I-4.3—To work through education, research, and advocacy toward an environmentally safe world in which all children receive health care, food, and shelter; are nurtured; and live free from violence in their home and their communities.

I-4.4—To work through education, research, and advocacy toward a society in which all young children have access to high-quality early care and education programs.

I-4.5—To work to ensure that appropriate assessment systems, which include multiple sources of information, are used for purposes that benefit children.

I-4.6—To promote knowledge and understanding of young children and their needs. To work toward greater societal acknowledgment of children's rights and greater social acceptance of responsibility for the well-being of all children.

I-4.7—To support policies and laws that promote the well-being of children and families, and to work to change those that impair their well-being. To participate in developing policies and laws that are needed, and to cooperate with other individuals and groups in these efforts.

I-4.8—To further the professional development of the field of early childhood care and education and to strengthen its commitment to realizing its core values as reflected in this Code.

Principles (Individual)

P-4.1—We shall communicate openly and truthfully about the nature and extent of services that we provide.

P-4.2—We shall apply for, accept, and work in positions for which we are personally well-suited and professionally qualified. We shall not offer services that we do not have the competence, qualifications, or resources to provide.

P-4.3—We shall carefully check references and shall not hire or recommend for employment any person whose competence, qualifications, or character makes him or her unsuited for the position.

P-4.4—We shall be objective and accurate in reporting the knowledge upon which we base our program practices.

P-4.5—We shall be knowledgeable about the appropriate use of assessment strategies and instruments and interpret results accurately to families.

P-4.6—We shall be familiar with laws and regulations that serve to protect the children in our programs and be vigilant in ensuring that these laws and regulations are followed.

P-4.7—When we become aware of a practice or situation that endangers the health, safety, or well-being of children, we have an ethical responsibility to protect children or inform parents and/or others who can.

P-4.8—We shall not participate in practices that are in violation of laws and regulations that protect the children in our programs.

P-4.9—When we have evidence that an early childhood program is violating laws or regulations protecting children, we shall report the violation to appropriate authorities who can be expected to remedy the situation.

P-4.10—When a program violates or requires its employees to violate this Code, it is permissible, after fair assessment of the evidence, to disclose the identity of that program.

Principles (Collective)

P-4.11—When policies are enacted for purposes that do not benefit children, we have a collective responsibility to work to change these practices.

P-4.12—When we have evidence that an agency that provides services intended to ensure children's well-being is failing to meet its obligations, we acknowledge a collective ethical responsibility to report the problem to appropriate authorities or to the public. We shall be vigilant in our follow-up until the situation is resolved.

P-4.13—When a child protection agency fails to provide adequate protection for abused or neglected children, we acknowledge a collective ethical responsibility to work toward the improvement of these services.

NAEYC has taken reasonable measures to develop the Code in a fair, reasonable, open, unbiased, and objective manner, based on currently available data. However, further research or developments may change the current state of knowledge. Neither NAEYC nor its officers, directors, members, employees, or agents will be liable for any loss, damage, or claim with respect to any liabilities, including direct, special, indirect, or consequential damages incurred in connection with the Code or reliance on the information presented.

STATEMENT OF COMMITMENT*

As an individual who works with young children, I commit myself to furthering the values of early childhood education as they are reflected in the ideals and principles of the NAEYC Code of Ethical Conduct. To the best of my ability I will

- Never harm children.

- Ensure that programs for young children are based on current knowledge and research of child development and early childhood education.

- Respect and support families in their task of nurturing children.

- Respect colleagues in early childhood care and education and support them in maintaining the NAEYC Code of Ethical Conduct.

- Serve as an advocate for children, their families, and their teachers in community and society.

- Stay informed of and maintain high standards of professional conduct.

- Engage in an ongoing process of self-reflection, realizing that personal characteristics, biases, and beliefs have an impact on children and families.

- Be open to new ideas and be willing to learn from the suggestions of others.

- Continue to learn, grow, and contribute as a professional.

- Honor the ideals and principles of the NAEYC Code of Ethical Conduct.

GLOSSARY OF TERMS RELATED TO ETHICS

Code of Ethics Defines the core values of the field and provides guidance for what professionals should do when they encounter conflicting obligations or responsibilities in their work.

---

*This Statement of Commitment is not part of the Code but is a personal acknowledgement of the individual's willingness to embrace the distinctive values and moral obligations of the field of early childhood care and education. It is recognition of the moral obligations that lead to an individual becoming part of the profession.

Values Qualities or principles that individuals believe to be desirable or worthwhile and that they prize for themselves, for others, and for the world in which they live.

Core Values Commitments held by a profession that are consciously and knowingly embraced by its practitioners because they make a contribution to society. There is a difference between personal values and the core values of a profession.

Morality Peoples views of what is good, right, and proper; their beliefs about their obligations; and their ideas about how they should behave.

Ethics The study of right and wrong, or duty and obligation, that involves critical reflection on morality and the ability to make choices between values and the examination of the moral dimensions of relationships.

Professional Ethics The moral commitments of a profession that involve moral reflection that extends and enhances the personal morality practitioners bring to their work, that concern actions of right and wrong in the workplace, and that help individuals resolve moral dilemmas they encounter in their work.

Ethical Responsibilities Behaviors that one must or must not engage in. Ethical responsibilities are clear-cut and are spelled out in the Code of Ethical Conduct (for example, early childhood educators should never share confidential information about a child or family with a person who has no legitimate need for knowing).

Ethical Dilemma A moral conflict that involves determining appropriate conduct when an individual faces conflicting professional values and responsibilities.

SOURCES FOR GLOSSARY TERMS AND DEFINITIONS

Feeney, S., & N. Freeman. 1999. *Ethics and the early childhood educator: Using the NAEYC code.* Washington, DC: NAEYC.

Kidder, R.M. 1995. *How good people make tough choices: Resolving the dilemmas of ethical living.* New York: Fireside.

Kipnis, K. 1987. How to discuss professional ethics. *Young Children* 42 (4): 26–30.

Reprinted by permission. NAEYC Position Statement (2005). Code of ethical conduct and statement of commitment. Washington, DC: Author. Downloaded from http://www.naeyc.org/about/positions/pdf/PSETH05.PDF.

CASE STUDY: USING THE CODE OF ETHICAL CONDUCT

Ashley is a teacher in an early intervention program for infants and toddlers. As part of her job, she works with families in both the center-based program and in their homes. Ashley has a Bachelor's degree in early childhood special education, nine years of experience as a classroom teacher, and has recently begun a Master's program. In addition, she has cared for three foster children who experienced developmental delays because of exposure to a prenatal terratogen, such as alcohol.

Ashley is currently working with a group of 8 children ranging in age from 5 to 29 months. She loves the family-style grouping, or mixed-age grouping, because she is able to work with each child and family for 3 years. This continuity of care has proven to be important to developing a trusting relationship with families. Each person knows that they will be together for a long period of time; so much effort is placed on honestly communicating and resolving differences.

Right now, she is working with a family—mother, grandmother, and older toddler, Josie, who has spinal bifida. Up until about six months ago, the infant was assessed to be developmentally delayed in her physical and social development and on-developmental level for her cognitive and emotional skills. However, the two most current developmental assessments demonstrated cause for concern regarding her cognitive skills. Ashley has been in constant communication with the family about these results. Josie's grandmother, Helen, shows a desire to modify the IFSP (Individualize Family Service Plan). Josie's mother, Cora, will not discuss the results. When the topic is brought up, she changes the subject. During one home visit, she stated that "Josie is normal, and I refuse to believe that she is retarded." Ashley tried to explain what it meant to be cognitively delayed. She provided specific examples and tried to be empathetic by acknowledging the hurt and disappointment that Cora must have been feeling. Cora ended the visit early, stating that she had another commitment.

Ashley knew that Cora was hurting and that she might just need some time and space for reflection, so Cora promptly left. Ashley knew that this wasn't typical behavior for Cora; she usually fully participates in discussions and does whatever is agreed to be best for Josie. Ashley began to wonder what additional support she could provide.

When Helen brought Josie to the center the next day, she reported that Cora left after dinner and had not returned home. Helen had called friends, but could not locate her. Ashley could tell that she was visibly worried. Helen reported that Cora had not done this since right before Josie was born. She speculated if Cora had "fallen off the wagon" after being sober for almost two and a half years. This was the first that Ashley had heard of this. She wondered if Cora's reaction to the assessment was connected. If it was, how should she address it?

Use the following statements/questions to respond to this case.

1. Record your first reactions to this case.

2. Who is involved in the case? How are they affected by the situation?

3. What are the issues facing those involved?

4. What solutions can you generate for this case? Don't evaluate them; just list them.

5. Overlap each solution in #4 with the Code of Ethical Conduct.

6. Which solution will you select that reflects an appropriate course of action given the Code? Why are you selecting this solution?

Find a colleague and ask that person to read and respond to this case. Have a meeting to compare your responses. In what ways are they similar? Different? What can you learn from the way your colleague approached and solved this dilemma?

Additional resources regarding becoming a professional early childhood educator include the following:

Berthelsen, D., Brownlee, J., & Boulton-Lewis, G. (2002). Caregivers' epistemological beliefs in toddler programs. *Early Child Development and Care, 172,* 503–516.

Brophy-Herb, H. E., Kostelnik, M. J., & Stein, L. C. (2001). A developmental approach to teaching about ethics using the NAEYC Code of Ethical Conduct. *Young Children, 56*(1), 80–84.

Buell, M. J., Pfister, I., & Gamel-McCormick, M. (2002). Caring for the caregiver: Early Head Start/family child care partnerships. *Infant Mental Health Journal, 23*(1–2), 213–230.

NAEYC (2004, November). Resources for exploring the ethical dimensions of the early childhood profession. *Beyond the Journal: Young Children on the Web.* Retrieved from http://www.journal.naeyc.org.

Recchia, S. L., & Loizou, E. (2002). Becoming an infant caregiver: Three profiles of personal and professional growth. *Journal of Research in Childhood Education, 16,* 133–147.

GETTING STARTED

When starting in a new position working with children, there is always a cadre of information to learn. Use this fill-in-the-blank section to customize this resource book to your specific environment.

What are the school's or center's hours of operation?

On school days: _____

_____

_____

On vacation days: _____

_____

_____

What is the basic daily schedule and what are my responsibilities during each of those time segments?

_____

_____

_____

_____

_____

_____

_____

What are the procedures for checking children in and out of the program?

_____

_____

_____

_____

Do I call if I must be absent? Who is my contact?

Name _____

Phone number_____

What is the dress code for employees?

_____

_____

_____

For what basic health and safety practices will I be responsible? Where are the materials stored for this?

Sanitizing tables: _____

_____

_____

_____

Cleaning and maintaining equipment and materials (bleach, gloves, and so on):__

_____

_____

_____

What are the emergency procedures?

Mildly injured child: _____

_____

_____

_____

_____

Earthquake/tornado: _____

_____

_____

_____

_____

Fire: _____

_____

_____

_____

_____

First aid: _____

_____

_____

_____

Other: _____

_____

_____

_____

_____

CHILD DEVELOPMENT

Whether you are working with infants, toddlers, preschoolers, or primary-aged children, a teacher's first requirement is to know how children develop and learn. In your college program, you no doubt studied child development. Learning about child development, however, is an ongoing process because new patterns are constantly being discovered and understood by researchers. In addition, as you work with more and more children, you will better understand universal or typical patterns of development as well as unique or individual patterns of development. This section provides you with a shortened version of the universal steps most infants and toddlers go through as they develop. Some children will move easily from one step to another, but other children move forward in one area and lag behind in others. Use these milestones as a guide for arranging an environment or planning activities in your room. To further assist with your thinking about applying your knowledge of child development to your classroom practices, articles about primary caregiving and continuity of care are included.

DEVELOPMENTAL MILESTONES*

PHYSICAL DEVELOPMENT						
Birth to 3 Months	4 to 6 Months	7 to 9 Months	10 to 12 Months	13 to 18 Months	19 to 24 Months	25 to 36 Months
Acts reflexively—sucking, stepping, rooting	Holds cube in hand	Sits independently	Supports entire body weight on legs	Builds tower of two cubes	Walks up stairs independently, one step at a time	Maneuvers around obstacles in a pathway
	Reaches for objects with one hand	Stepping reflex returns, so that child bounces when held	Walks when hands are held	Turns the pages of a cardboard book two or three at a		Runs in a more adult-like fashion; knees are slightly

PHYSICAL DEVELOPMENT, continued						
Birth to 3 Months	**4 to 6 Months**	**7 to 9 Months**	**10 to 12 Months**	**13 to 18 Months**	**19 to 24 Months**	**25 to 36 Months**
		on a surface in a standing position		time		bent, arms move in the opposite direction
Swipes at objects in front of body, uncoordinated	Rolls from back to side	Leans over and reaches when in a sitting position	Cruises along furniture or steady objects	Scribbles vigorously	Jumps in place	Walks down stairs independently
Holds head erect and steady when lying on stomach	Reaches for objects in front of body, coordinated	Gets on hands and knees but may fall forward	Stands independently	Walks proficiently	Kicks a ball	Marches to music
Lifts head and shoulders	Sits with support	Crawls	Walks independently	Walks while carrying or pulling a toy	Runs in a modified fashion	Uses feet to propel wheeled riding toys
Rolls from side to back	Transfers objects from hand to hand	Pulls to standing position	Crawls up stairs or steps	Walks up stairs with assistance	Shows a decided preference for one hand	Rides a tricycle
Follows moving objects with eyes	Grabs objects with either hand	Claps hands together	Voluntarily releases objects held in hands		Completes a three-piece puzzle with knobs	Usually uses whole arm movements to paint or color
	Sits in tripod position using arms for support	Stands with adult's assistance	Has good balance when sitting; can shift positions without falling		Builds a tower of six cubes	Throws ball forward, where intended

(*continued*)

PHYSICAL DEVELOPMENT, continued

Birth to 3 Months	4 to 6 Months	7 to 9 Months	10 to 12 Months	13 to 18 Months	19 to 24 Months	25 to 36 Months
		Learns pincer grasp, using thumb with forefinger to pick up objects	Takes off shoes and socks			Builds tower using eight or more blocks
		Uses finger and thumb to pick up objects				Imitates drawing circles and vertical and horizontal lines
		Brings objects together with banging noises				Turns pages in book one by one
						Fingers work together to scoop up small objects
						Strings large beads on a shoelace

LANGUAGE AND COMMUNICATION DEVELOPMENT

Birth to 3 Months	4 to 6 Months	7 to 9 Months	10 to 12 Months	13 to 18 Months	19 to 24 Months	25 to 36 Months
Communicates with cries, grunts, and facial expressions	Babbles spontaneously	Varies babble in loudness, pitch, and rhythm	Uses preverbal gestures to influence the behavior of others	Has expressive vocabulary of 10 to 20 words	Continues using telegraphic speech	Continues using telegraphic speech combining three or four words
Prefers human voices	Acquires sounds of native language in babble	Adds *d, t, n,* and *w* to repertoire of babbling sounds	Demonstrates word comprehension skills	Engages in "jargon talk"	Is able to combine three words	

LANGUAGE AND COMMUNICATION DEVELOPMENT, continued						
Birth to 3 Months	**4 to 6 Months**	**7 to 9 Months**	**10 to 12 Months**	**13 to 18 Months**	**19 to 24 Months**	**25 to 36 Months**
Coos	Uses canonical, systematic consonant-vowel pairings; babbling occurs	Produces gestures to communicate, often by pointing	Waves good-bye	Engages in telegraphic speech by combining two words together	Talks, 25 percent of words are understandable	Speaks in complete sentences following word order of native language
Laughs	Participates in interactive games initiated by adults	May say *mama* or *dada* but does not connect words with parents	Speaks recognizable first word	Experiences a burst of language development	Refers to self by name	Displays effective conversational skills
Smiles and coos to initiate and sustain interactions with caregiver	Takes turns while interacting		Initiates familiar games with adults	Comprehends approximately 50 words	Joins three or four words into a sentence	Refers to self as *me* or *I* rather than by name
					Comprehends approximately 300 words	Talks about objects and events not immediately present
					Expressive language includes a vocabulary of approximately 250 words	Uses grammatical markers and some plurals
						Vocabulary increases rapidly, up to 300 words

(*continued*)

LANGUAGE AND COMMUNICATION DEVELOPMENT, continued						
Birth to 3 Months	**4 to 6 Months**	**7 to 9 Months**	**10 to 12 Months**	**13 to 18 Months**	**19 to 24 Months**	**25 to 36 Months**
						Enjoys being read to if allowed to participate by pointing, talking, and turning pages
COGNITIVE DEVELOPMENT						
Cries for assistance	Recognizes people by their voices	Enjoys looking at books with familiar objects	Solves sensorimotor problems by deliberately using schemas, such as shaking a container to empty its contents	Explores properties of objects by acting on them in novel ways	Points to and identifies objects on request, such as when reading a book, touring, and so on	Uses objects for purposes other than intended
Acts reflexively	Enjoys repeating acts, such as shaking a rattle, that produce results in the external world	Distinguishes familiar from unfamiliar faces	Points to body parts upon request	Solves problems through trial and error	Sorts by shapes and colors	Uses private speech while working
Prefers to look at patterned objects, bull's-eye, horizontal stripes, and the human face	Searches with eyes for source of sounds	Engages in goal-directed behavior	Drops toys intentionally and repeatedly looks in the direction of the fallen object	Experiments with cause-and-effect relationships such as turning on televisions, banging on drums, and so on	Recognizes self in photographs and mirror	Classifies objects based on one dimension, such as toy cars versus blocks

COGNITIVE DEVELOPMENT, continued

Birth to 3 Months	4 to 6 Months	7 to 9 Months	10 to 12 Months	13 to 18 Months	19 to 24 Months	25 to 36 Months
Imitates adults' facial expressions	Enjoys watching hands and feet	Anticipates events	Waves good-bye	Plays body identification games	Demonstrates deferred imitation	Follows two-step directions
Searches with eyes for sources of sounds	Searches for a partially hidden object	Finds objects that are totally hidden	Shows evidence of stronger memory capabilities	Imitates novel behaviors of others	Engages in functional play	Concentrates or attends to self-selected activities for longer periods of time
Begins to recognize familiar people at a distance	Uses toys in a purposeful manner	Imitates behaviors that are slightly different than those usually performed	Follows simple, one-step directions	Identifies family members in photographs	Finds objects that have been moved while out of sight	Points to and labels objects spontaneously, such as when reading a book
Discovers and repeats bodily actions such as sucking, swiping, and grasping	Imitates simple actions	Begins to show interest in filling and dumping containers	Categorizes objects by appearance		Solves problems with internal representation	Coordinates pretend play with other children
Discovers hands and feet as extension of self	Explores toys using existing schemas such as sucking, banging, grasping, shaking, and so on		Looks for objects hidden in a second location		Categorizes self and others by gender, race, hair color, and so on	Gains a nominal sense of numbers through counting and labeling objects in a set

(continued)

COGNITIVE DEVELOPMENT, continued

Birth to 3 Months	4 to 6 Months	7 to 9 Months	10 to 12 Months	13 to 18 Months	19 to 24 Months	25 to 36 Months
						Begins developing concepts about opposites such as big and small, tall and short, in and out
						Begins developing concepts about time such as today, tomorrow, and yesterday

SOCIAL DEVELOPMENT

Birth to 3 Months	4 to 6 Months	7 to 9 Months	10 to 12 Months	13 to 18 Months	19 to 24 Months	25 to 36 Months
Turns head toward a speaking voice	Seeks out adults for play by crying, cooing, or smiling	Becomes upset when separated from a favorite adult	Shows a decided preference for one or two caregivers	Demands personal attention	Shows enthusiasm for company of others	Observes others to see how they do things
Recognizes primary caregiver	Responds with entire body to familiar face by looking at the person, smiling, kicking legs, and waving arms	Acts deliberately to maintain the presence of a favorite adult by clinging or crying	Plays parallel to other children	Imitates behaviors of others	Views the world only from own, egocentric perspective	Engages primarily in solitary or parallel play
Bonds to primary caregiver	Participates actively in interactions with others	Uses adults as a base for exploration, typically	Enjoys playing with siblings	Becomes increasingly aware of the self as a	Plays contently alone or near adults	Sometimes offers toys to other children

SOCIAL DEVELOPMENT, continued						
Birth to 3 Months	4 to 6 Months	7 to 9 Months	10 to 12 Months	13 to 18 Months	19 to 24 Months	25 to 36 Months
	by vocalizing in response to adult speech			separate being		
Finds comfort in the human face	Smiles at familiar faces and stares solemnly at strangers	Looks to others who are exhibiting signs of distress	Begins asserting self	Shares affection with people other than primary caregiver	Engages in functional play	Begins to play cooperatively with other children
Displays a social smile	Distinguishes between familiar and unfamiliar adults and surroundings	Enjoys observing and interacting briefly with other children	Begins developing a sense of humor	Shows ownership of possessions	Defends possessions	Engages in sociodramatic play
Is quieted by a voice		Likes to play and responds to games such as pat-a-cake and peek-a-boo	Develops a sense of self-identity through the identification of body parts	Begins developing a view of self as autonomous when completing tasks independently	Recognizes self in photographs or mirrors	Wants to do things independently
Begins to differentiate self from caregiver		Engages in solitary play	Begins distinguishing boys from girls		Refers to self with pronouns such as *I* or *me*	Asserts independence by using *no* a lot
		Develops preferences for particular people and objects			Categorizes people by using salient characteristics such as race or hair color	Develops a rudimentary awareness that others have wants or feelings that may be different than his/her own

(*continued*)

SOCIAL DEVELOPMENT, continued

Birth to 3 Months	4 to 6 Months	7 to 9 Months	10 to 12 Months	13 to 18 Months	19 to 24 Months	25 to 36 Months
		Shows distress when in the presence of a stranger			Shows less fear of strangers	Makes demands of or "bosses" parents, guardians, and caregivers
						Uses physical aggression less and uses words to solve problems
						Engages in gender stereotypical behavior

EMOTIONAL DEVELOPMENT

Birth to 3 Months	4 to 6 Months	7 to 9 Months	10 to 12 Months	13 to 18 Months	19 to 24 Months	25 to 36 Months
Feels and expresses three basic emotions: interest, distress, and disgust	Expresses delight	Responds to social events by using the face, gaze, voice, and posture to form coherent emotional patterns	Continues to exhibit delight, happiness, discomfort, anger, and sadness	Exhibits autonomy by frequently saying *no*	Expresses affection to others spontaneously	Experiences increase in number of fears
Cries to signal a need	Responds to the emotions of caregivers	Expresses fear and anger more often	Expresses anger when goals are blocked	Labels several emotions	Acts to comfort others in distress	Begins to understand the consequences of basic emotions
Quiets in response to being held, typically	Begins to distinguish familiar from unfamiliar people	Begins to regulate emotions through moving into or out of experiences	Expresses anger at the source of frustration	Connects feelings with social behaviors	Shows the emotions of pride and embarrassment	Learns skills for coping with strong emotions

EMOTIONAL DEVELOPMENT, continued						
Birth to 3 Months	**4 to 6 Months**	**7 to 9 Months**	**10 to 12 Months**	**13 to 18 Months**	**19 to 24 Months**	**25 to 36 Months**
Feels and expresses enjoyment	Shows a preference for being held by a familiar person	Begins to detect the meaning of others' emotional expressions	Begins to show compliance to caregivers' requests	Begins to understand complicated patterns of behavior	Uses emotion words spontaneously in conversations or play	Seeks to communicate more feelings with specific words
Shares a social smile	Begins to assist with holding a bottle	Looks to others for cues on how to react	Often objects to having playtime stopped	Demonstrates the ability to communicate needs	Begins to show sympathy to another child or adult	Shows signs of empathy and caring
Reads and distinguishes adults' facial expressions	Expresses happiness selectively by laughing and smiling more with familiar people	Shows fear of strangers	Begins eating with a spoon	May say *no* to something he/she wants	Becomes easily hurt by criticism	Loses control of emotions and throws temper tantrums
Begins to self-regulate emotional expressions			Assists in dressing and undressing	May lose emotional control and have temper tantrums	Experiences a temper tantrum when goals are blocked, on occasion	Able to recover from temper tantrums
Laughs aloud			Acts in loving, caring ways toward dolls or stuffed animals, typically	Shows self-conscious emotions such as shame, guilt, and shyness	Associates facial expressions with simple emotional labels	Enjoys helping with chores such as cleaning up toys or carrying grocery bags
Quiets self by using techniques such as sucking a thumb or pacifier			Feeds self a complete meal when served finger foods	Becomes frustrated easily		Begins to show signs of being ready for toileting

(*continued*)

EMOTIONAL DEVELOPMENT, continued						
Birth to 3 Months	4 to 6 Months	7 to 9 Months	10 to 12 Months	13 to 18 Months	19 to 24 Months	25 to 36 Months
			Claps when successfully completes a task			Desires that routines be carried out exactly as has been done in the past

*The developmental milestones listed are based on universal patterns of when various traits emerge. Because each child is unique, certain traits may develop at an earlier or later age.

CONTINUITY OF CARE IN THE EARLY YEARS? MULTIPLE AND CHANGEABLE CHILD CARE ARRANGEMENTS IN AUSTRALIA

Continuity of care is seen as an important aspect of quality child care for children in the early years of life. Yet previous studies suggest that up to a third of Australian children in their first three years attend two or more care settings a week. A new study shows that use of multiple child care arrangements, and changes in care arrangements, are relatively common. What are the implications for the quality of care experienced by children?

Continuity of care in the early years of life has been seen as an essential component of good quality child care. There has been a growing unease in the early childhood field, however, about the threat to continuity of care for young children posed by children's experience of many caregivers during their first three years. In particular, the phenomena of multiple child care arrangements (more than one regular care arrangement per week) and changeable child care (shifts over time in care arrangements) are seen as increasing problems.

There is a concern among early childhood professionals that good practice may not be enough to ensure quality care when children receive mixed or unstable caregiving arrangements. This concern was the impetus for the *Child Care Choices* study.

Multiple and changeable child care arrangements are certainly becoming more prevalent. A recent study in New South

Wales (Goodfellow, 1999) suggests that over 30 percent of one-year-old children experience multiple child care arrangements. Similarly, a Victorian study showed that 57 percent of two-year-olds attended two early childhood services a day, a "substantial" number in three services a day, with some participating in up to four services on several days of the week (Rodd, 1996). In the United States, the Study of Early Child Care, conducted by the National Institute for Child and Human Development (NICHD), found that over the first year of life, almost all infants were in more than two care arrangements, with over a third (37 percent) in three or more nonmaternal child care arrangements.

This pattern tends to increase as children get older. In their longitudinal study of 145 children, Harrison and Ungerer (2000) recorded the number of changes of care that children experienced from birth to age six. Over this period a third of children had experienced highly changeable child care—an average of 12 different arrangements with a range of 9 to 15.

What is less clear from these studies are the reasons why parents use mixed child care arrangements, or change the care arrangements for their child. Goodfellow's (1999) research suggested that the high cost of care and lack of available care were major factors in parents' use of multiple arrangements. On the other hand, Ochiltree and Edgar (1995) reported that parents used varied settings because of changing family circumstances or wanting to maximize the quality of the child's care. Harrison and Ungerer (1997, 2002) found that many mothers preferred to leave their infants with someone they felt comfortable with and could trust—such as their husband, grandparents, close relative, or friend. As a result of this preference, and perhaps the limited availability of these alternative carers, babies received care from a number of different adults. Thus, it is not clear from existing research how much control parents feel they have over their choice of child care arrangements.

Although previous studies have alerted us to the possible negative outcomes of multiple and changeable child care, to date no Australian research has set out to investigate this specific phenomenon.

It is helpful, however, to summarize the existing indications of risk that have been associated with multiple and changeable care. Negative outcomes for children have been reported in some studies. In Goodfellow's (1999) study, 42 percent of parents of children in multiple child care arrangements said that their children showed negative behavior in child care. The children were reported as being confused or lost in the group, being tired or unhappy, and having difficulty forming relationships. It should be noted, however, that this information was derived only from parents' reports, which may have involved some bias. Similarly, the American-based NICHD Early Child Care Research Network (1998), which used objective indicators of children's outcomes, reported that children who had experienced a number of different child care arrangements in the first two years exhibited more problem behaviors than children who had been in fewer child care arrangements.

Some research indicates that multiple child care arrangements may also be associated with problem outcomes for children. For example, studies have found that multiple and changeable child care is associated with lower intelligence scores (Whitebook, Howes, and Phillips, 1990), poorer social relationships (Howe and Stewart, 1987), and more insecure attachment with mothers (Harrison and Ungerer, 1997). Harrison and Ungerer (2000) also noted that when there was a pattern of changeable care across the first six years of life, children were rated as having more behavioral problems in their first year of school.

Child Care Choices Study

These questions about the impact of multiple and changeable child care on children's development are the subject of a three-year investigation conducted by a team of researchers from Macquarie University, the Australian Institute of Family Studies, and Charles Sturt University. The study is funded by the Australian Research Council (ARC) and the New South Wales Department of Community Services under an ARC Linkage grant.

Data from the first year of the study allow us to report on the extent of multiple and changeable child care arrangements in the current sample of 363 parents from urban and rural New South Wales, the reasons parents have given for their choice of child care arrangements for their children, and their satisfaction with current care arrangements.

For the purpose of the study, multiple child care arrangements were defined as arrangements involving two or more concurrent nonmaternal child care arrangements on a regular basis across seven days.

Location of Sample
It was expected that the issues surrounding multiple and changeable care were likely to be context specific. In particular, there were indications from existing studies (for example, Goodfellow, 1999) that availability of care was more problematic for families living in regional and rural areas, compared to metropolitan areas. On the other hand, some regional centers offer a coordinated, multi-purpose approach to child care, compared to city services, which tend to be single purpose.

It was unclear whether these differing conditions might be associated with different patterns of multiple or changeable child care arrangements. Thus, to shed light on these potential differences, an important aim of the research was to include a range of child care services, across urban and rural locations.

Description of Sample
At the time of writing, 42 centers (22 urban, 20 rural) and seven family child care schemes (three urban, four rural) have agreed to participate in the study. A total of 363 parents (167 urban, 196 rural) recruited through the centers and the schemes have completed a CATI telephone interview. The main parental carer of the study child participated in the telephone interview. Over 90 percent of respondents were mothers of the children concerned.

Of the parents, the majority of mothers (78 percent) and fathers (79 percent) were Australian born. Of those who were born outside Australia, 13 percent of mothers and 12 percent of fathers were from English-speaking countries (Great Britain, Canada, America, New Zealand), 5 percent of mothers and 4 percent of fathers were from Asia, 1 percent of mothers and 1 percent of fathers were from South America, and 1 percent of mothers and 3 percent of fathers were from Europe. There was thus some under-representation of immigrants.

Mothers represented a varied group in terms of age (mean age 33.6 years) and education (35 percent had completed secondary school to Year 9, 10, or 12; 25 percent had a tertiary diploma or trade qualification; and 39 percent had a university or postgraduate degree). Fathers tended to be several years older than mothers and had similar levels of education. This was thus, on average, a fairly highly educated sample.

The families came from a range of household income levels, with about half of the sample earning gross annual household incomes of $70,000 and over. Most of the parents were in paid work (78 percent of mothers and 97 percent of fathers). There was thus, on average, a fairly high socioeconomic status among families.

Differences were noted between urban and rural parents on several demographic measures. Rural mothers were on average younger than urban mothers (mean age of 32.1 years for rural mothers and 35.4 years for urban mothers), were more likely to have been born in Australia (94.2 percent rural mothers compared to 62.3 percent of urban mothers), and were less well educated (23.2 percent of rural mothers with university degrees compared to 54.9 percent of urban mothers). Similar differences in characteristics were evident for fathers from rural and urban areas.

Mothers and fathers in rural areas worked a similar number of hours in paid work as their urban counterparts, with mothers working an average of 30.3 hours a week and fathers working an average of 47.0 hours per week. There were significant differences between urban and rural families in annual gross household income although there was an extremely wide variation in reported income in each location (mean income of $61,622 for rural families, and $101,710 for urban families). Family size ranged from one to five children. Forty percent of the children were only children in the family and 53 percent were first-borns. Rural families tended to be larger than urban families, with 28 percent of rural families having three or more children compared to 7 percent of urban families.

The focus of this study was on children aged three years and under. Of the 363 children (183 boys, 180 girls), 23 (6 percent) were aged under less than 12 months old, 113 (31 percent) were aged one to two years, and 209 (58 percent) were aged two to three years. A further 18 children were aged three years or older. Information regarding these children is included in the total group analyses.

Procedures
Recruitment occurred through child care centers and family child care schemes. After gaining approval from management, research assistants approached parents as they collected their children and invited them to participate in the study. Interested parents

completed a one-page "Expression of Interest" form, listing their child's weekly child care arrangements. Selection of participants was based on achieving similar numbers of children in each of the three age groups (0–1, 1–2, and 2–3 years), equally distributed across urban and rural settings.

Selected families were followed up with a CATI telephone interview about the family and the child care history of the child, including changes of care. Parents were asked about their satisfaction with current child care arrangements and their reasons for using multiple care settings or for changing care arrangements. (Extensive data on child and child care settings were also collected, but will be the subject of later publications.)

Results
The results from the telephone interview with parents are presented first for incidence of multiple child care arrangements. This is followed by an analysis of parents' reasons for using multiple child care arrangements and their satisfaction with current arrangements. The incidence of changeable care in the sample is presented next along with an analysis of parents' reasons for changing child care arrangements over the previous 12-month period.

Incidence of multiple child care arrangements
Results show that 45 percent of the families were using two or more regular weekly child care arrangements for their children. The range was one to five settings but most multiple care use involved two settings (see Table 1). The proportion of children

TABLE 1 Numbers and Percentages of Children Experiencing Single and Multiple Child Care by Location ($n = 363$)

No. of Care Settings	Urban		Rural		Total	
	n	%	n	%	n	%
1	93	55.7	107	54.6	200	55.1
2	56	33.5	67	34.2	123	33.9
3	15	9.0	19	9.7	34	9.4
4	2	1.2	3	1.5	5	1.4
5	1	0.6	0	0	1	0.3
Total	167		196		363	
Multiple care	74	44.3	89	45.4	163	44.9

TABLE 2   **Total Number of Child Care Arrangements by Age of Child (*n* = 295)**

No. of Arrangements	Children Aged 0–1		Children Aged 1–2		Children Aged 2–3	
	n	%	*n*	%	*n*	%
1	17	73.9	63	56.8	87	54.4
2	4	17.4	40	36.0	53	32.5
3	2	8.7	6	5.4	18	11.3
4	0		1	0.9	3	1.9
5	0		1	0.9	0	
Total	23		111		161	
Total multiple care	6	26.1	48	43.2	73	45.3

experiencing multiple child care arrangements was similar for urban (44 percent) and rural children (45 percent).

Multiple child care arrangements were common at all ages with some increase in use according to the age of the child. The current care arrangements of children in the sample shown in Table 2 indicate that, on average, 26.1 percent of children were under 12 months old, with less than 10 percent reported as being in three or more child care settings a week at this age.

Because these data were based on only 23 children, retrospective reports were examined about the care history of the one- to two-year-olds and the two- to three-year-olds in the sample during their first year. Similar results were found: 31 percent of the 271 children had experienced multiple child care arrangements in their first year, with 7.7 percent having experienced three or more settings.

For children currently in their second year, 43.2 percent were in multiple care arrangements, with 7.2 percent in three or more arrangements. The percentages of children in multiple care arrangements were very similar in the third year with 45.3 percent in multiple care arrangements and 13.2 percent in three or more care settings a week (see Table 2).

Parents reported that, in addition to the main long child care or family child care setting, most used the child's father, grandparents or relatives, friends, babysitters, or nannies as regular care providers.

TABLE 3   Type of Care Used by Families in Urban and Rural Settings (*n* = 362)

Type of Care	Urban (*n* = 167)		Rural (*n* = 195)		Total (*n* = 362)	
	n	%	*n*	%	*n*	%
Long child care only	66	39.5	93	47.7	159	43.9
Family child care only	27	16.2	13	6.7	40	11.0
More than 1 formal care	7	4.2	11	5.6	18	5.0
Formal + father	27	16.2	23	11.8	50	13.8
Formal + informal	29	17.4	45	23.1	74	20.4
Formal + informal + father	11	6.6	10	5.1	21	5.8
Total	167	100	195	100	362	100

Note: Formal care refers to long child care and family child care. Informal care refers to care by nonparental family, friends, and paid babysitters or nannies.

Table 3 shows the different patterns of care arrangements used by families in urban and rural areas. No differences were found between care used in the two locations. In both locations, the largest percentages of children were in formal care only, reflecting the recruitment of the sample from long child care and family child care (approximately 55 percent in both urban and rural areas).

Combinations of formal and informal care were more common than more than one form of formal care for the children under three years of age (20 percent used a combination of formal and informal care, and only 5 percent used more than one form of formal care such as two long child care centers or a long child care centre and family child care). Table 3 shows that combinations of care that involved regular weekly care by fathers were used in 38 urban families (23 percent) and 33 rural families (17 percent).

Grandparents played a major role in the informal care of young children aged under one year, although the use of different kinds of informal care, in addition to grandparents, became more frequent as children became older.

Reasons for Using Multiple Child Care Arrangements

Parents were given a number of possible reasons for using multiple care and asked to rate the extent to which each of these applied to them on a scale of 1 (does not apply) to 5 (definitely applies).

TABLE 4   Means and Standard Deviations of Parent Ratings of Reasons for Making Multiple Child Care Arrangements (on a scale from 1 = does not apply, to 5 = definitely applies) ($n = 163$)

Reason	Mean	(SD)
1. It is good for my child to experience a center environment and a family environment.	4.3	(1.2)
2. I like my child to be able to interact with different adults and children.	4.2	(1.3)
3. The arrangements are convenient for me.	4.2	(1.2)
4. I want my child to spend some time with his/her family members.	4.1	(1.5)
5. I want my child to have a range of experiences so he/she will learn new things.	3.9	(1.4)
6. I don't think it is good for my child to be in formal care only.	3.5	(1.6)
7. I don't think it is good for my child to stay in one type of care all the time.	3.2	(1.5)
8. My child will not get the stimulation he/she needs in one type of child care.	2.7	(1.6)
9. It is hard to find child care available during the times I need it.	2.6	(1.7)
10. My preferred child care arrangement is not consistently available.	2.1	(1.6)
11. I cannot afford to use my preferred child care arrangement all the time.	2.0	(1.5)
12. I can't access enough hours of care in my preferred child care arrangement.	2.0	(1.6)
13. The family keeps moving, and I am unable to keep my child in a stable routine.	1.2	(0.7)

Results showed that parents were more likely to agree with statements about benefits for the child than those about other reasons such as difficulty accessing appropriate or preferred child care (see Table 4). Statements relating to benefits for the child included: "to have a range of experiences and learn new things," "to spend time with family members," and "to be able to interact with different adults and children." Parents using multiple child care arrangements also agreed that it was not good for their child to attend formal care only.

Convenience was a common reason for parents choosing multiple care; reasons such as affordability and lack of availability of preferred child care arrangements, were less salient for parents (see Table 4). Comparisons between the urban and rural samples, using t-tests, showed no difference on these items between the two groups.

Two factors emerged from a principal components analysis of parents' responses to the 13 reasons. Factor 1, labeled "out of parents' control," included five reasons related to affordability and availability of child care and constant moving of the family that made multiple child care arrangements necessary. Items 9–13 in Table 4 had high loadings on this factor, and when treated as a scale, had an alpha reliability of .63.

Factor 2, labeled "parents' choice," included eight reasons based on what parents considered was good for their child. Parents consistently reported that the set of reasons reflecting their own choice applied more than "out of parents' control" reasons. Items 1–8 in Table 4 had high loadings on this factor, and when treated as a scale, had an alpha reliability of .79.

No differences were found on these two factors between parents of children from the three age groups, between parents with different levels of multiple child care arrangements (two care settings compared with three or more), between (five) different income levels, or between parents from different locations (rural and urban). Thus, while the sample had above average income, income did not appear to be a factor affecting use of multiple child care arrangements.

Satisfaction with Care

Parents were asked to rate their levels of satisfaction with their overall weekly child care arrangements, using a scale of 1 (not at all satisfied) to 5 (very satisfied). Typically, parents were very satisfied with the care they were using (mean satisfaction: 4.4).

This was true for primary care settings (95 percent very satisfied); additional care arrangements (second care setting—96 percent very satisfied); and third, fourth, and fifth care settings (100 percent very satisfied for each). There were no differences between rural and urban samples in reported satisfaction with care.

Incidence of Changes in Care

Approximately a quarter of the parents ($n = 93$, 26 percent) said they had changed their child's care arrangements during the past 12 months. Of these, most (87 percent) reported one change only, with two or more changes reported as relatively rare.

Changes of carers within the same care setting had occurred for more than one third of children (38 percent) with staff turnover

TABLE 5　Reasons for Change of Child Care Arrangements ($n = 93$)

Reason for Change	Yes		No	
	n	(%)	*n*	(%)
1. The child care was more conveniently located.	37	39.8	56	60.2
2. The previous child care arrangement became unavailable.	37	39.8	56	60.2
3. The child care was better quality.	26	28.0	67	72.0
4. The care setting wasn't suited to the child.	18	19.4	75	80.6
5. The child care was more affordable.	17	18.3	76	81.7
6. There were problems with the service (e.g., change of management, conflict).	17	18.3	76	81.7

in services given as the major reason (63 percent of the 136 parents who reported this kind of change). An increase in the number of child care arrangements was reported as a change by 17 percent of parents and a decrease in number of arrangements by only 8 percent.

Reasons for Changing Care Arrangements

Parents were given six possible reasons for making changes in care arrangements and asked to rate on a 5-point scale the extent to which the reasons applied to them and the extent to which they felt they had control over several kinds of change in care arrangements.

Table 5 shows that the four most common reasons for changing care were to move to a more convenient location, because a previous arrangement was unavailable, problems with the service, and to obtain better quality care. Affordability of care was not a common reason for making a change.

Parents reported that most changes (changes in place and increases or decreases in the number of care arrangements, or hours of care) were definitely a result of their choice. The only change that parents reported as out of their control was a change in caregiver, usually a result of changes or staff turnover in a service.

Conclusions

This paper reports preliminary findings on 363 families from the longitudinal *Child Care Choices Study* that examines the effects of multiple and changeable child care arrangements on the development of young children.

This sample is somewhat advantaged (on average), but analyses suggested that socioeconomic factors were not critical determinants of reasons for use of multiple and changeable child care. Nevertheless, sample characteristics mean we should not generalize these findings to the broader population. Since the key interest of the study is in child outcomes in relation to care experiences, the socioeconomic issues are less critical than for a straightforward "prevalence" study.

Results from the first year of data collection indicate that use of multiple care arrangements is relatively common, with 45 percent of respondents reporting weekly use of two or more care settings. Parents also reported a reasonably high rate of changes in child care arrangements over the previous 12 months, with 26 percent reporting one or more changes in care for their child. The incidence of multiple and changeable child care arrangements was similar for urban and rural samples despite differences between the two locations in family characteristics, notably income.

The high level of satisfaction reported by parents with their child's care is consistent with the results of other studies on child care satisfaction in Australia (Greenblatt and Ochiltree, 1993) and internationally (Pungello and Kurt-Costes, 1999; Peyton, Jacobs, O'Brien, and Roy, 2001). It was notable that parents reported that the changes in care over the previous year were, with the exception of changes in carer, the result of their own choice and felt to be within their control.

The reasons parents gave for the particular mix of care arrangements they had for their child indicated that arrangements were usually made according to what parents felt was best for their child. These findings are contrary to the suggestion made in the Goodfellow (1999) report, that multiple care arrangements were largely the result of factors beyond the control of parents (such as the availability and accessibility of child care). These latter factors, however, were the main reasons given for changes in child care arrangements. According to these parents, children were most likely to change the place they went to child care because the new arrangement was more convenient for parents or because the previous arrangement became unavailable. Changes in carer were likely to be the result of staff turnover in children's services.

If continuity of care is seen to be an important part of quality care for children and an essential base for further learning and development, there may be a cause for concern in these findings. In the crucial first three years of life, nearly half of the children in the *Child Care Choices Study* are having the experience on a weekly basis of two or more caregivers in addition to the care of the parent who is their main caregiver at home. A quarter of children have also experienced at least one change in care over the previous year. The findings suggest that while many of the multiple child care arrangements are made through parental choice, commonly because parents believe that their decisions are in the best interests of their child, the changes made to care arrangements are due largely to factors outside parental control.

Whether or not these threats to continuity of care do make any difference to children's development is an issue still open to investigation. It is a key question for this study as it follows the children, their families, and caregivers over the next two years.

References

Goodfellow, J. (1999), "Multicare arrangement patchworks: The multiple use of formal and informal care in NSW," Report for New South Wales Department of Community Services, Office of Child Care, Sydney.

Greenblatt, E. & Ochiltree, G. (1993), *Use and Choice of Child Care,* AIFS Early Childhood Study Paper, no. 4, Australian Institute of Family Studies, Melbourne.

Harrison, L. J. & Ungerer, J. A. (2002), "Maternal employment predictors of infant—mother attachment security at 12 months postpartum," *Developmental Psychology,* vol. 38, no. 5, pp. 758–773.

Harrison, L. J. & Ungerer, J. A. (2000), "Children and child care: A longitudinal study of the relationships between developmental outcomes and use of non-parental care from birth to six," Panel Data and Policy Conference, Canberra, May.

Harrison, L. J. & Ungerer, J. A. (1997), "Child care predictors of infant—mother attachment security at age 12 months," *Early Child Development and Care,* vol. 137, pp. 31–46.

Howes, C. (1990), "Can the age of entry into child care and the quality of child care predict adjustment in kindergarten?" *Developmental Psychology,* vol. 26, pp. 292–303.

Howes, C. & Hamilton, C. E. (1993), "The changing experience of child care: Changes in teachers and in teacher—child relationships and children's social competence with peers," *Early Childhood Research Quarterly,* vol. 8, pp. 15–32.

Howes, C. & Stewart, P. (1987), "Child's play with adults, peers, and toys: An examination of family and child care influences," *Developmental Psychology,* vol. 23, pp. 423–430.

NICHD Early Child Care Research Network (2000), "The relation of child care to language and cognitive development," *Child Development,* vol. 71, pp. 960–980.

NICHD Early Child Care Research Network (1998), "Early child care and self-control, compliance, and problem behavior at twenty-four and thirty-six months," *Child Development,* vol. 69, pp. 1145–1170.

NICHD Early Child Care Research Network (1996), "Characteristics of infant care: Factors contributing to positive caregiving," *Early Childhood Research Quarterly,* vol. 11, pp. 269–306.

Ochiltree, G. & Edgar, D. (1995), *Today's Child Care, Tomorrow's Children,* AIFS Early Childhood Study Paper, no. 7. Australian Institute of Family Studies, Melbourne.

Peisner-Feinberg, E. S., Burchinal, M. R., Clifford, R. M., Culkin, M. L., Howes, C., Kagan, S. L., & Yazejian, N. (2001), "The relation of pre-school child care quality to children's cognitive and social developmental trajectories through second grade," *Child Development,* vol. 72, pp. 1534–1553.

Peyton, Y., Jacobs, A., O'Brien, M. & Roy, C. (2001), "Reasons for choosing child care: Associations with family factors, quality and satisfaction," Early *Childhood Research Quarterly,* vol. 16, pp. 191–208.

Pungello, E. P. & Kurt-Costes, B. (1999), "Why and how working women choose child care: A review with a focus on infancy," *Developmental Review,* vol. 19, pp. 31–96.

Rodd, J. (1996), "A week in the life of a four-year old: A study of Victorian children's patterns of usage of early childhood services," *Australian Journal of Early Childhood,* vol. 21, pp. 37–42.

Sparrow, S. S., Balla, D. A., & Cicchetti, D. (1984), "Vineland Adaptive Behaviour Scales Interview Edition Survey Form Manual," American Guidance Service, Circle Pines.

Whitebook, M., Howes, C., & Phillips, D. (1990), "Who cares? Child care teachers and the quality of care in America: Final report of the National Child Care Staffing Study," Child Care Employee Project, Oakland, CA.

Authors: **Jennifer Bowes**, Macquarie University; **Sarah Wise**, Australian Institute of Family Studies; **Linda Harrison**, Charles Sturt University; **Ann Sanson**, Australian Institute of Family Studies; **Judy Ungerer**, Macquarie University; **Johanna Watson**, Macquarie University; **Tracey Simpson**, Charles Sturt University. The authors thank **Jenny Cohen** for assistance with data analysis.

Reprinted by permission from Australian Institute of Family Studies. Bowes, J., Wise, S., Harrison, L., Sanson, A., Ungerer, J., Watson, J., & Simpson, T. (2003). Continuity of care in the early years? Multiple and changeable child care arrangements in Australia. *Family Matters*, *64*, p. 30–35.

PRIMARY CAREGIVING ARTICLE

After reading the article about ways parents organize caregiving for their children, use these questions to assist with your reflections.

1. In your program, what families use more than one caregiver concurrently? What do you think are the reasons for this decision?

2. What information can you provide to family members to help them consider the developmental needs of very young children? Or what support can you or your program provide to decrease the need for multiple caregivers?

For additional resources related to child and brain development, as well as continuity of care, consider reading:

Bernhardt, J. L. (2000). A primary caregiving system for infants and toddlers: Best for everyone involved. *Young Children, 55*(2), 74–80.

Edwards, C. P., & Raikes, H. (2002). Extending the dance: Relationship-based approaches to infant/toddler care and education. *Young Children, 57*(4), 10–17.

Gallagher, K. C. (2005). Brain research and early childhood development: A Primer for developmentally appropriate practice. *Young Children, 60*(4), 12–18, 20.

Gunnar, M. R., & Cheatam, C. L. (2003). Brain and behavior interface: Stress and the developing brain. *Infant Mental Health Journal, 24*(3), 195–211.

Kovach, B. A., & De Ros, D. A. (1998). Respectful, individual, and responsive caregiving for infants: The key to successful care in group settings. *Young Children, 53*(3), 61–64.

Miller, K. (1999, September). Caring for the little ones: Continuity of care. *Child Care Information Exchange,* 94–97.

Oppenheim, D., & Koren-Karie, N. (2002). Mothers' insightfulness regarding their children's internal worlds: The capacity underlying secure child-mother relationships. *Infant Mental Health Journal, 23*(6), 593–605.

Vaught, M. (2001). Caregivers' Corner. Another look at brain research. *Young Children, 56*(4), 33.

MATERIALS FOR CHILDREN

Children construct their own understanding of the world around them as they interact with appropriate materials and with other people. Teachers play an important role in providing choices of good-quality playthings that match children's developmental abilities and interests. When budgets are limited, teachers must be able to select toys and materials that provide optimum learning opportunities. Creative teachers learn how to "scrounge" for toys and how to make playthings out of recycled materials. The lists that follow suggest materials that are priorities for children at particular levels of development.

FOR YOUNG INFANTS (BIRTH THROUGH SIX MONTHS)

- unbreakable mirrors that can be attached low on walls or near changing tables and cribs

- stuffed, washable toys or rag dolls, with stitched faces and eyes

- mobiles and visuals hung out of reach

- grasping toys: simple rattles, squeeze toys, keys on ring, clutch or texture balls

- hanging toys for batting

- wrist or ankle bells

- you—the most important toy that very young infants have is you! Spend time talking, singing, and interacting with the infant.

FOR OLDER, MOBILE INFANTS (7 THROUGH 12 MONTHS)

- soft rubber animals for grasping

- simple one-piece vehicles 6–8 inches, with large wheels

- grasping toys for skill development: toys on suction cups, stacking rings, nesting cups, squeeze toys, plastic pop beads, bean bags, busy boxes

- containers and objects to fill and dump

- small cloth, plastic, and board books

- soft cloth or foam blocks for stacking

- simple floating objects for water play

- balls of all kinds, including some with special effects

- low, soft climbing platforms

- large unbreakable mirrors

- recorded music and songs

FOR TODDLERS (ONE TO THREE YEARS)

For Fine Motor Skills

- nesting materials

- sand and water play toys, such as funnels, colanders, small sand tools

- simple activity boxes, with doors, lids, switches; more complex after about 18 months: turning knob or key

- pegboards with large pegs

- four- to five-piece stacking materials

- pop beads and stringing beads

- Duplo-type plastic interlocking blocks for stacking, building

- simple three- to five-piece puzzles with knobs, familiar shapes for younger toddlers; add more complicated puzzles as the children demonstrate competencies

- simple matching materials

- books, including tactile books, cloth, plastic, board picture, and story books

- clay, crayons, nontoxic paint, pencils, markers, and a variety of paper for expressing ideas

- science materials, such as magnifying glass, color paddles, and objects from the natural world, including pets

For Gross Motor Skills

- push and pull toys

- simple doll carriages and wagons

- replications of adult tools for pushing and pretend play, such as lawn mower, shopping cart

- stable riding toys with four wheels and no pedals for younger toddlers; tricycles for older toddlers who are ready

- balls of all sizes

- large cardboard boxes for crawling through, painting on, or hiding in

- tunnels for crawling through

- tumbling mats and low climbing platforms

- large, hollow wooden and unit blocks

- stationary outdoor climbing equipment designed for toddlers

- slides and ladders made for toddlers or positioned on the ground

- outdoor building materials, tires, and other loose parts

For Pretend Play

- small wood or plastic people and animal figures

- small cars and trucks

- dolls of various ethnic and gender appearance, with clothes and other accessories and furniture such as doll beds

- plastic dishes and pots and pans

- hats

- simple dress-up clothes or accessories (e.g., purse)

- telephones
- scarves and fabrics
- puppets

For Sensory Play

- recorded music and player
- play dough
- fingerpaint
- large nontoxic crayons
- sturdy paper
- simple musical instruments

Some ideas adapted from M. Bronson, *The Right Stuff for Children Birth to 8: Selecting Play Materials to Support Development.* Washington, DC: NAEYC, 1995.

Remember that recycled materials and other loose parts have many uses for exploration and creativity.

BASIC PROGRAM EQUIPMENT AND MATERIALS FOR AN EARLY CHILDHOOD CENTER

If you are responsible for ordering supplies for your classroom or early childhood program, the following guidelines will be useful.

INDOOR EQUIPMENT

The early childhood room should be arranged into well-planned areas of interest, such as the housekeeping and doll corner, block building area, and so on to encourage children to play in small groups throughout the playroom and engage in activities of their special interest rather than attempting to play in one large group.

The early childhood center must provide selections of indoor play equipment from all the following areas of interest. Selection should be of sufficient quantities so that children can participate in a wide range of activities. Many pieces of equipment can be home-made. Consider the age and developmental levels of the children when making selections.

Playroom Furnishings

- Tables: seat four to six children (18 inches high for three-year-olds, 20–22-inches high for four- and five-year-olds)

- Chairs: 10 inches high for three-year-olds, 12–14 inches high for four- and five-year-olds

- Open shelves: 26 inches high, 12 inches deep, 12 inches between shelves

- Lockers: 12 inches wide, 12 inches deep, 32–36 inches high

Housekeeping or Doll Corner

Item	Number Recommended for 10 Children
Dolls	3
Doll clothes	Variety
Doll bed—should be large enough for a child to get into, bedding	1
Doll high chair	1
Small table, four chairs	1 set
Tea party dishes	6-piece set with tray
Stove: child size, approximately 24 × 23 × 12 inches	1
Sink: child size, approximately 24 × 23 × 12 inches	1
Refrigerator: child size, approximately 28 × 23 × 12 inches	1
Pots and pans, empty food cartons, measuring cups, spoons, and so on	Variety
Mop, broom, dustpan	1
Ironing board and iron	1
Clothespins and clothesline	1
Toy telephones	2
Dress-up box—men's and women's hats, neckties, pocketbooks, shoes, old dresses, scarves, jewelry, and so on	Variety
Mirror	1

Art Supplies

Item	Number Recommended for 10 Children
Newsprint paper 18 × 24 inches	1 ream
Colored paper—variety	3 packages
Large crayons	10 boxes
Tempera paint—red, yellow, blue, black, white	1 can each
Long-handled paintbrushes: making a stroke from ½ inch to 1 inch wide	10–12
Easels	1
Fingerpaint paper: glazed paper such as shelf, freezer, or butcher's paper	1 roll
Paste	1 quart
Blunt scissors	10
Collage: collection of bits of colored paper, cut-up gift wrappings, ribbons, cotton, string, scraps of fabric, and so on for pasting	Variety

(*continued*)

Art Supplies, continued

Item	Number Recommended for 10 Children
Magazines for cutting and pasting	Variety
Clay: play dough	50 pounds
Cookie cutters, rolling pins	Variety

Block Building Area

Item	Number Recommended for 10 Children
Unit blocks—purchased or homemade (directions are available)	276 pieces, 11 shapes
Large, lightweight blocks	Variety
Small wooden or rubber animals and people	Variety
Small trucks, airplanes, cars, and boats	12
Medium airplanes	3
Medium boats	2
Medium-sized trucks: 12 to 24 inches	3

Manipulative Toys

Item	Number Recommended for 10 Children
Wooden inlay puzzles, approximately 5 to 20 pieces	6
Color cone	1
Nested blocks	1
Pegboards, variety of shapes and sizes	1
Large spools and beads for stringing	2 sets
Toys that have parts that fit into one another	2
Lotto games	2
Dominoes	1

Music Corner

- record player, tape player, CD player
- suitable records, tapes, and CDs
- rhythm instruments
- dress-up scarves for dancing

Books and Stories

A carefully selected book collection (20–30 books) for the various age levels should include the following categories:

- transportation, birds and animals, family life
- community helpers, science, nonsense rhymes
- Mother Goose rhymes, poems, and stories
- homemade picture books
- collection of pictures classified by subject
- library books to enrich the collection

Nature Study and Science

- aquarium or fish bowls
- plastic materials
- magnifying glass, prism, magnet, thermometers
- growing indoor plants, garden plot
- stones, leaves, acorns, birds' nests, caterpillars, worms, tadpoles, and so on

Woodworking Center

Basic woodworking operations include the following:

- sanding
- gluing
- hammering
- holding (with a vise or clamp)
- fastening (with screws)
- drilling
- sawing

Materials for a woodworking center include the following:

- sturdy workbench (or table)
- woodworking tools: broad-headed nails ¾ to 1½ inches long; C-clamp or vise (to hold wood); flat-headed, 12-oz. hammer for beginning woodworking experiences, later a claw hammer may be added; 14-inch saw with 10 teeth to the inch

■ soft white pine lumber scraps (it is difficult to drive nails into hardwood; plywood is not suitable either); packing boxes of soft pine can be disassembled and used for hammering work.

Sand Play

In an outdoor area, sand should be confined so it does not get scattered over the rest of the playground. The area should be large enough so several children can move about without crowding each other. A 10- to 12-inch ledge around a sandbox can serve as a boundary and at the same time provide children with a working surface or a seat. If sand is about 6 to 8 inches below the top of the ledge, it is less likely to spill onto the playground. Sand should be about 18 inches deep so children can dig or make tunnels. For drainage, include 4 or 5 inches of gravel on the bottom of the sandbox.

Basic equipment: Ordinary plastic or metal kitchen utensils— cups, spoons, pails, shovels, sifters, funnels, scoops, bowls.

Water Play

Water play can be either an indoor or an outdoor activity, depending upon the climate. Clear plastic water basins can be used for water play. When they are on a stand with wheels, they can be moved easily to any area of a room. When these plastic containers are used, children have the advantage of being able to see through the sides and the bottom. If a table stands on a carpeted floor, a plastic runner can be used to protect the carpet, and spillage will not be a serious housekeeping problem.

Materials: Clear tubing, sponges, strainers, funnels, corks, pitchers, and measuring cups. For added interest, rotary beaters, spoons, small bowls, plastic basters, and straws.

OUTDOOR EQUIPMENT

The outdoor play equipment should be grouped according to use. For example, plan for both active and quiet play; allow for free areas for use of wheel toys. The following is a list of suggested basic outdoor play equipment for the early childhood program.

■ climbing structure(s)

■ large and small packing boxes

■ slides

- swings with canvas seats

- wagons and wheelbarrows

- pedal toys: tricycles, cars, and so on

- sandbox with spoons, shovels, pails, and so on

- balls

- a variety of salvage material, such as rubber tires, tire tubes, lengths of garden hose, ropes, and cardboard boxes, to enrich the play

Note: Many activities, such as housekeeping play and art activities, at times can be transferred to the outdoor area.

Use the following checklist to evaluate your playground setup.

☐ Pathways are clear and spacious between areas so that traffic flows well and equipment does not obstruct the movement of children.

☐ Space and equipment are organized so that children are readily visible and easily supervised by adults.

☐ Different types of activity areas are separated. (Tricycle paths are separate from swings; the sandbox is separate from the climbing area.)

☐ Open space is available for active play.

☐ Some space is available for quiet play.

☐ Dramatic play can be set up outdoors, as space is available.

☐ Art activities can be set up outdoors.

☐ A portion of the play area is covered for use in wet weather.

☐ A storage area is available for play equipment.

☐ A drinking fountain is available.

☐ The area has readily accessible restrooms.

OBSERVATION AND ASSESSMENT

This section begins by asking you to respond to the following questions:

1. What is your current approach to observing and recording the development and learning of very young children?

2. Infant and toddler teachers spend a great deal of their time assisting children with getting their basic needs met. What do you think you can learn about a child's development by observing these routine-care times, such as eating or diapering? Provide at least one specific example that covers two or three areas of development (i.e., physical, cognitive, language, social, and emotional).

A variety of tools can be used to assess children's development. Using assessment tools in conjunction with developmental milestones helps caregivers recognize a child's developmental accomplishments as well as determine the child's next growth steps. Not all children will give as much time to the teacher's directions. The teacher needs to observe each child to determine the level to which each child is performing independently and with assistance so that appropriately challenging instruction can begin. This knowledge is useful in planning curriculum, designing the room environment for success, and establishing appropriate behavior management techniques that help children manage their own behavior. No doubt your college practicum experience taught you the logistics of observing: using objective description and recording specific, dated, brief, and factual information. Observation can take many forms; the most common include the following:

- anecdotal records
- running records

- checklists

- time or event sampling

- authentic documentation, including photographs and videotapes

ANECDOTAL RECORDS

An **anecdotal record** is a brief narrative description of one event that is kept by the teacher while the child is performing a task. At first, this may seem daunting, but it will become part of your everyday routine. Keep a small spiral notebook and pen or pencil in your pocket. When a child begins an activity, watch what the child does and write down what you actually observe the child doing. Remember to use descriptive language (Marion, 2004) and report the facts and only the facts. As time permits, probably during nap time, the brief notes are turned into a full scenario so that anyone could read the record at a later date:

For example, the following notes were turned into a anecdotal record:

Notes: Xu cried 3 minutes; rocked, patted back, puppy, calmed

Anecdotal Record: Xu cried hard for 3 minutes after his mother left him in my care today. I asked if it was okay if I held him and he held up his hands. We sat in the rocking chair while he snuggled in my arms. He was comforted, as indicated by the ceasing of crying, by my patting his back and by holding his "puppy" (a stuffed animal) close to his cheek. He pointed to a truck on the floor after about 8 minutes of rocking and was put on the floor to push the truck back and forth.

ANECDOTAL RECORD

Child's Name: Antonio G.   Age: 1 yr. 5 mo.
Observer's Name: Victoria   Date: October 27, 2005
Setting: Indoors, coffee table

What actually happened/What I saw	Reflection/Interpretation/Questions
Antonio was sitting by the couch on the floor. Then he crawled over closer to the coffee table. He looked at the coffee table and pulled himself	He was so persistent! This is the first of pulling and standing that's been seen here at school. Antonio's grandmother reported that he has

(continued)

ANECDOTAL RECORD, continued

What actually happened/What I saw	Reflection/Interpretation/Questions
to a standing position by pushing both of his hands down on the table. He balanced, holding on, for 6 seconds before letting go. Antonio stood independently for about 3 seconds before loosing his balance and falling to a sitting position. He pulled himself to a standing position 7 more times before he crawled away from the area.	been doing this frequently at home in the evenings. It is exciting to see him advancing in physical skills after the car accident and his head injury. I wonder if this means he is back on track with his physical development. I should have his grandmother see about an appointment with his doctor to share this news.

ANECDOTAL RECORD

Child's Name: _____   Age: _____

Observer Name: _____   Date: _____

Setting: _____

What actually happened/What I saw	Reflection/Interpretation/Questions

ANECDOTAL RECORD

Child's Name: _____   Age: _____

Observer Name: _____   Date: _____

Setting: _____

What actually happened/What I saw	Reflection/Interpretation/Questions

RUNNING RECORD

Another form of authentic assessment is the running record, which covers a longer time span and gives more information than an anecdotal record. Often it may have a specific developmental focus such as "social interactions." A running record gives you information about other developmental areas because of its very detailed nature. This form of observation requires the caregiver to not be involved with children for several minutes while writing the observation. You will be setting yourself apart from the children and writing continuously, in as much detail as possible. You will write what the child does and says, by herself and in interactions with other people and materials. Use descriptive phrases (Marion, 2004) that are objective as previously described. Note that the format for this form of assessment is four columns. The left column is for writing contextual information, the middle columns include the behavioral observations of "what saw" and "what heard," while the right column is for interpretations, reflections, or questions that you are making about the observational data Remember to date all observations so you can notice developmental change over time.

RUNNING RECORD

Child's Name: Trish H.
Observer's Name: Jorge
Developmental Focus: Social interactions with peers

Age: 0 yr. 10 mo.
Date: December 12, 2005

Context	Behavioral Descriptions of Observations		Reflections/Interpretations/Questions
	What did I see?	What did I hear?	
9:05	Trish picked up a leopard-print piece of fabric and held it out to Megan. She smiled and looked directly at Megan while holding it out. Megan continued to look at her hands, which were holding a piece of fake fur. Trish began to vocalize loudly.	Aaah, mooomaamoo, gah, gah	She wants to interact with Megan. Using nonverbal cues to get her attention. When that doesn't work, she moves to another strategy, vocalization.

(continued)

RUNNING RECORD, continued

| Context | Behavioral Descriptions of Observations | | Reflections/Interpretations/Questions |
	What did I see?	What did I hear?	
Trish, Pepe, and Megan are sitting in the empty wading pool. They have all independently crawled in and are manipulating the fabric swatches that were placed there by my co-teacher.	Megan continues to look at her hands and the fur. Trish grins widely at Pepe and holds out the fabric. He smiles back and reaches for the fabric. Trish pulls it back and babbles with much expression.	Mee, mee, tob, tob, tob	Is she trying to say "Megan"?
9:11 Pepe crawls out the pool.	Trish crawls closer to Megan and grabs a hold of fabric close to Megan's foot. Megan squeals in delight and Trish joins in.	Weeee, weeee, meee	Again, she is initiating interaction with her peer.
			She sounds happy and angry at the same time. I wonder if she only wanted to *show* Pepe the fabric, not have him touch it.
			Sharing the fabric? At least enjoying being in the area together.

RUNNING RECORD

Child's Name: _____ Age: _____

Observer Name: _____ Date: _____

Development Focus: _____

| Context | Behavioral Descriptions of Observations | | Reflections/Interpretations/Questions |
	What did I see?	What did I hear?	

CHECKLIST

A checklist is often used as a means of assessment because it is one of the easiest assessment tools to use. A checklist consists of a predetermined list of developmental criteria for which the observer indicates "yes" or "no." The observer reads the developmental criteria and makes a checkmark if the decision is a "yes." The criteria should be clearly observable. This form of assessment requires that additional notes be recorded. Many teachers design their own checklists to fit the specific needs of their program. The following checklist is an example of one that might be used to assess the development of infants and toddlers.

Developmental Checklist

Child's Name: _____

Observer's Name: _____

Observation Date: _____

PHYSICAL DEVELOPMENT	OBSERVED	
Birth to 3 Months	**Date**	**Comments**
Acts reflexively—sucking, stepping, rooting		
Swipes at objects in front of body, uncoordinated		
Holds head erect and steady when lying on stomach		
Lifts head and shoulders		
Rolls from side to back		
Follows moving objects with eyes		
4 to 6 Months		
Holds cube in hand		
Reaches for objects with one hand		
Rolls from back to side		
Reaches for objects in front of body, coordinated		
Sits with support		
Transfers objects from hand to hand		
Grabs objects with either hand		
Sits in tripod position using arms for support		
7 to 9 Months		
Sits independently		
Stepping reflex returns, so that child bounces when held on a surface in a standing position		
Leans over and reaches when in a sitting position		
Gets on hands and knees but may fall forward		
Crawls		
Pulls to standing position		
Claps hands together		
Stands with adult's assistance		
Learns pincer grasp, using thumb with forefinger to pick up objects		
Uses finger and thumb to pick up objects		
Brings objects together with banging noises		

PHYSICAL DEVELOPMENT, continued	OBSERVED	
10 to 12 Months	Date	Comments
Supports entire body weight on legs		
Walks when hands are held		
Cruises along furniture or steady objects		
Stands independently		
Walks independently		
Crawls up stairs or steps		
Voluntarily releases objects held in hands		
Has good balance when sitting; can shift positions without falling		
Takes off shoes and socks		
13 to 18 Months		
Builds tower of two cubes		
Turns the pages of a cardboard book two or three at a time		
Scribbles vigorously		
Walks proficiently		
Walks while carrying or pulling a toy		
Walks up stairs with assistance		
19 to 24 Months		
Walks up stairs independently, one step at a time		
Jumps in place		
Kicks a ball		
Runs in a modified fashion		
Shows a decided preference for one hand		
Completes a three-piece puzzle with knobs		
Builds a tower of six cubes		
25 to 36 Months		
Maneuvers around obstacles in a pathway		
Runs in a more adult-like fashion; knees are slightly bent, arms move in the opposite direction		
Walks down stairs independently		
Marches to music		
Uses feet to propel wheeled riding toys		

(*continued*)

PHYSICAL DEVELOPMENT, continued	OBSERVED	
25 to 36 Months	Date	Comments
Rides a tricycle		
Usually uses whole arm movements to paint or color		
Throws a ball forward, where intended		
Builds tower using eight or more blocks		
Imitates drawing circles and vertical and horizontal lines		
Turns pages in book one by one		
Fingers work together to scoop up small objects		
Strings large beads on a shoelace		

Additional Observations for Physical Development
The developmental milestones listed are based on universal patterns of when various traits emerge. Because each child is unique, certain traits may develop at an earlier or later age.

LANGUAGE AND COMMUNICATION DEVELOPMENT	OBSERVED	
Birth to 3 Months	Date	Comments
Communicates with cries, grunts, and facial expressions		
Prefers human voices		
Coos		
Laughs		
Smiles and coos to initiate and sustain interactions with caregiver		
4 to 6 Months		
Babbles spontaneously		
Acquires sounds of native language in babble		
Canonical, systematic consonant-vowel pairings; babbling occurs		
Participates in interactive games initiated by adults		
Takes turns while interacting		
7 to 9 Months		
Varies babble in loudness, pitch, and rhythm		
Adds *d*, *t*, *n*, and *w* to repertoire of babbling sounds		
Produces gestures to communicate often by pointing		
May say *mama* or *dada* but does not connect words with parents		

LANGUAGE AND COMMUNICATION DEVELOPMENT, continued	OBSERVED	
10 to 12 Months	Date	Comments
Uses preverbal gestures to influence the behavior of others		
Demonstrates word comprehension skills		
Waves good-bye		
Speaks recognizable first word		
Initiates familiar games with adults		
13 to 18 Months		
Has expressive vocabulary of 10 to 20 words		
Engages in "jargon talk"		
Engages in telegraphic speech by combining two words together		
Experiences a burst of language development		
Comprehends approximately 50 words		
19 to 24 Months		
Continues using telegraphic speech		
Able to combine three words		
Talks, 25 percent of words being understandable		
Refers to self by name		
Joins three or four words into a sentence		
Comprehends approximately 300 words		
Expressive language includes a vocabulary of approximately 250 words		
25 to 36 Months		
Continues using telegraphic speech combining three or four words		
Speaks in complete sentences following word order of native language		
Displays effective conversational skills		
Refers to self as *me* or *I* rather than by name		
Talks about objects and events not immediately present		
Uses grammatical markers and some plurals		

(*continued*)

LANGUAGE AND COMMUNICATION DEVELOPMENT, continued	OBSERVED	
25 to 36 Months	Date	Comments
Vocabulary increases rapidly, up to 300 words		
Enjoys being read to if allowed to participate by pointing, talking, and turning pages		

Additional Observations for Cognitive Development

The developmental milestones listed are based on universal patterns of when various traits emerge. Because each child is unique, certain traits may develop at an earlier or later age.

COGNITIVE DEVELOPMENT	OBSERVED	
Birth to 3 Months	Date	Comments
Cries for assistance		
Acts reflexively		
Prefers to look at patterned objects, bull's-eye, horizontal stripes, and the human face		
Imitates adults' facial expressions		
Searches with eyes for sources of sounds		
Begins to recognize familiar people at a distance		
Discovers and repeats bodily actions such as sucking, swiping, and grasping		
Discovers hands and feet as extension of self		
4 to 6 Months		
Recognizes people by their voice		
Enjoys repeating acts, such as shaking a rattle, that produce results in the external world		
Searches with eyes for source of sounds		
Enjoys watching hands and feet		
Searches for a partially hidden object		
Uses toys in a purposeful manner		
Imitates simple actions		
Explores toys using existing schemas such as sucking, banging, grasping, shaking, and so on		
7 to 9 Months		
Enjoys looking at books with familiar objects		
Distinguishes familiar from unfamiliar faces		

COGNITIVE DEVELOPMENT, continued	OBSERVED	
7 to 9 Months	Date	Comments
Engages in goal-directed behavior		
Anticipates events		
Finds objects that are totally hidden		
Imitates behaviors that are slightly different from those usually performed		
Begins to show interest in filling and dumping containers		
10 to 12 Months		
Solves sensorimotor problems by deliberately using schemas, such as shaking a container to empty its contents		
Points to body parts upon request		
Drops toys intentionally and repeatedly looks in the direction of the fallen object		
Waves good-bye		
Shows evidence of stronger memory capabilities		
Follows simple, one-step directions		
Categorizes objects by appearance		
Looks for objects hidden in a second location		
13 to 18 Months		
Explores properties of objects by acting on them in novel ways		
Solves problems through trial and error		
Experiments with cause-and-effect relationships such as turning on televisions, banging on drums, and so on		
Plays body identification games		
Imitates novel behaviors of others		
Identifies family members in photographs		
19 to 24 Months		
Points to and identifies objects on request, such as when reading a book, touring, and so on		
Sorts by shapes and colors		
Recognizes self in photographs and mirror		
Demonstrates deferred imitation		

(*continued*)

COGNITIVE DEVELOPMENT, continued	OBSERVED	
19 to 24 Months	**Date**	**Comments**
Engages in functional play		
Finds objects that have been moved while out of sight		
Solves problems with internal representation		
Categorizes self and others by gender, race, hair color, and so on		
25 to 36 Months		
Uses objects for purposes other than intended		
Uses private speech while working		
Classifies objects based on one dimension, such as toy cars versus blocks		
Follows two-step directions		
Concentrates or attends to self-selected activities for longer periods of time		
Points to and labels objects spontaneously, such as when reading a book		
Coordinates pretend play with other children		
Gains a nominal sense of numbers through counting and labeling objects in a set		
Begins developing concepts about opposites such as big and small, tall and short, in and out		
Begins developing concepts about time such as today, tomorrow, and yesterday		

Additional Observations for Cognitive Development

The developmental milestones listed are based on universal patterns of when various traits emerge. Because each child is unique, certain traits may develop at an earlier or later age.

SOCIAL DEVELOPMENT	OBSERVED	
Birth to 3 Months	**Date**	**Comments**
Turns head toward a speaking voice		
Recognizes primary caregiver		
Bonds to primary caregiver		
Finds comfort in the human face		
Displays a social smile		
Is quieted by a voice		
Begins to differentiate self from caregiver		

SOCIAL DEVELOPMENT, continued	OBSERVED	
4 to 6 Months	Date	Comments
Seeks out adults for play by crying, cooing, or smiling		
Responds with entire body to familiar face by looking at a person, smiling, kicking legs, and waving arms		
Participates actively in interactions with others by vocalizing in response to adult speech		
Smiles at familiar faces and stares solemnly at strangers		
Distinguishes between familiar and nonfamiliar adults and surroundings		
7 to 9 Months		
Becomes upset when separated from a favorite adult		
Acts deliberately to maintain the presence of a favorite adult by clinging or crying		
Uses adults as a base for exploration, typically		
Looks to others who are exhibiting signs of distress		
Enjoys observing and interacting briefly with other children		
Likes to play and responds to games such as pat-a-cake and peek-a-boo		
Engages in solitary play		
Develops preferences for particular people and objects		
Shows distress when in the presence of a stranger		
10 to 12 Months		
Shows a decided preference for one or two caregivers		
Plays parallel to other children		
Enjoys playing with siblings		
Begins asserting self		
Begins developing a sense of humor		
Develops a sense of self-identity through the identification of body parts		
Begins distinguishing boys from girls		
13 to 18 Months		
Demands personal attention		
Imitates behaviors of others		

(continued)

SOCIAL DEVELOPMENT, continued	OBSERVED	
13 to 18 Months	**Date**	**Comments**
Becomes increasingly aware of the self as a separate being		
Shares affection with people other than primary caregiver		
Shows ownership of possessions		
Begins developing a view of self as autonomous when completing tasks independently		
19 to 24 Months		
Shows enthusiasm for company of others		
Views the world only from own, egocentric perspective		
Plays contentedly alone or near adults		
Engages in functional play		
Defends possessions		
Recognizes self in photographs or mirrors		
Refers to self with pronouns such as *I* or *me*		
Categorizes people by using salient characteristics such as race or hair color		
Shows less fear of strangers		
25 to 36 Months		
Observes others to see how they do things		
Engages primarily in solitary or parallel play		
Sometimes offers toys to other children		
Begins to play cooperatively with other children		
Engages in sociodramatic play		
Wants to do things independently		
Asserts independence by using *no* a lot		
Develops a rudimentary awareness that others have wants or feelings that may be different than their own		
Makes demands of or "bosses" parents, guardians, and caregivers		
Uses physical aggression less and uses words to solve problems		
Engages in gender stereotypical behavior		

Additional Observations for Social Development

The developmental milestones listed are based on universal patterns of when various traits emerge. Because each child is unique, certain traits may develop at an earlier or later age.

EMOTIONAL DEVELOPMENT	OBSERVED	
Birth to 3 Months	**Date**	**Comments**
Feels and expresses three basic emotions: interest, distress, and disgust		
Cries to signal a need		
Quiets in response to being held, typically		
Feels and expresses enjoyment		
Shares a social smile		
Reads and distinguishes adults' facial expressions		
Begins to self-regulate emotional expressions		
Laughs aloud		
Quiets self by using techniques such as sucking a thumb or pacifier		
4 to 6 Months		
Expresses delight		
Responds to the emotions of caregivers		
Begins to distinguish familiar from unfamiliar people		
Shows a preference for being held by a familiar person		
Begins to assist with holding a bottle		
Expresses happiness selectively by laughing and smiling more with familiar people		
7 to 9 Months		
Responds to social events by using the face, gaze, voice, and posture to form coherent emotional patterns		
Expresses fear and anger more often		
Begins to regulate emotions through moving into or out of experiences		
Begins to detect the meaning of others' emotional expressions		
Looks to others for clues on how to react		
Shows fear of strangers		
10 to 12 Months		
Continues to exhibit delight, happiness, discomfort, anger, and sadness		

(continued)

EMOTIONAL DEVELOPMENT, continued	OBSERVED	
10 to 12 Months	Date	Comments
Expresses anger when goals are blocked		
Expresses anger at the source of frustration		
Begins to show compliance to caregivers' requests		
Often objects to having playtime stopped		
Begins eating with a spoon		
Assists in dressing and undressing		
Acts in loving, caring ways toward dolls or stuffed animals, typically		
Feeds self a complete meal when served finger foods		
Claps when successfully completing a task		
13 to 18 Months		
Exhibits autonomy by frequently saying *no*		
Labels several emotions		
Connects feelings with social behaviors		
Begins to understand complicated patterns of behavior		
Demonstrates the ability to communicate needs		
May say *no* to something he/she wants		
May lose emotional control and have temper tantrums		
Shows self-conscious emotions such as shame, guilt, and shyness		
Becomes frustrated easily		
19 to 24 Months		
Expresses affection to others spontaneously		
Acts to comfort others in distress		
Shows the emotions of pride and embarrassment		
Uses emotion words spontaneously in conversations or play		
Begins to show sympathy to another child or adult		
Becomes easily hurt by criticism		
Experiences a temper tantrum when goals are blocked, on occasion		
Associates facial expressions with simple emotional labels		

As mentioned, an **event sampling** is similar, but the teacher looks at events instead of being directed by a timer. The teacher zeros in on an event and writes down all things that she sees pertaining to the event. For example, Barb has noticed that some of the toddlers in her room become particularly upset during diapering. Some of her event-sampling notes include the following:

- While helping Naomi onto changing table, the teacher notices that she clutching a large plastic peg close to her chest. The teacher removes it while telling Naomi that she doesn't want the toy to get dirty. Naomi begins to cry quietly.

- Dakota protests, by screaming, his having to stop building in order to have his diaper changed.

- James is dressing up in a hat and teacher tells him that he will need to have his diaper changed. She asks if he wants to do it now or after Julio. James replies, "Now" while walking toward the changing area.

AUTHENTIC DOCUMENTATION

This form of assessment involves taking **photographs or digital recordings** of the children and organizing the data using documentation panels. A documentation panel includes visual images and, whenever possible, narratives of dialogue that occurred during the experience that was documented. The goal of creating documentation panels is to make visible to you, the children, and family members the development and learning that has been occurring in the classroom. This method can be used for children of all ages and ability levels.

SYSTEMATIC OBSERVATION

Infant and toddler teachers spend a great deal of time observing and recording their observations of the children. Creating a plan for gathering data on all areas of development over time using a variety of tools can be a challenge. However, if you begin to think about this aspect of your work systematically, it can make this task easier (Marion, 2004). Many teachers create a list of all of the data they are gathering or want to gather as a way to manage their observations. A list may look like the following:

- Anecdotal records three times a week for each infant and two times a week for toddlers

- Running records one time a month for all of the children

- Developmental checklist two times a month for each infant and 1 time a month for toddlers

- Event and time sampling, other checklists and rating scales as needed

Assessment and observation may seem overwhelming as you begin your career in early childhood education. Do not shy away from it. Take the challenge and begin to look for the positive aspects of learning and mastering a new skill. Picture yourself as a student in your classroom and imagine what it is like to perfect something your teacher has just asked you to do. How does it make you feel? Now begin.

REFERENCE NOTED IN THIS SECTION

Marion, M. (2004). *Using observation in early childhood education.* Upper Saddle River, NJ: Pearson Merrill Prentice Hall.

Additional Articles about Assessment

Aytch, L. S., Castro, D. C., & Selz-Campbell, L. (2004). Early intervention services assessment scale (EISAS)—Conceptualization and development of a program quality self-assessment instrument. *Infants and Young Children, 17*(3), 236–246.

Cooney, M.H., & Buchanan, M. (2001). Documentation: Making assessment visible. *Young Exceptional Children, 4*(3), 10–16.

Dichtelmiller, M. L. (2004). Experiences from the field: New insights into infant/toddler assessment. *Young Children, 59*(1), 30–33.

Evangelista, N., & McLellan, M. J. (2004). The Zero to Three diagnostic system: A framework for considering emotional and behavioral problems in young children. *School Psychology Review, 33*(1), 159–173.

Gray, H. (2001). Initiation into documentation: A fishing trip with toddlers. *Young Children, 56*(1), 84–91.

INFANTS AND TODDLERS WITH SPECIAL NEEDS

Often, our assessment data provide evidence of unique patterns of development. In other words, the data show that an infant or toddler's development is following a course other than is typically expected. The child, for example, may be developing quicker, slower, or in a different pattern than most other children her age. Infant and toddler teachers play a particularly important role in identifying children with special needs because the earlier interventions can occur, the more effect they can have. Quickly evaluating and responding to developmental data can often result in improving development outcomes in the long run. Deciding on interventions or methods for modifying curriculum typically will involve a team of professionals, rather than just you. For that reason, you should make yourself familiar with resources in your community. First Steps is a federally funded intervention service that has programs in all states. Most states further divide the area into regions so that families have better access to services.

Additional resources about working with children with special needs include the following:

Birckmayer, J., Cohen, J., Jensen, I. D., & Variano, D. A. (2005). Kyle lives with his granny—Where are his mommy and daddy? *Young Children, 60*(3), 100–104.

Edmiaston, R., Dolezal, V., Doolittle, S., Erickson, C., & Merritt, S. (2000). Developing individualized education programs for children in inclusive settings: A developmentally appropriate framework. *Young Children, 55*(4), 36–41.

Odom, S.L., Teferra, T., & Kaul, S. (2004). An overview of international approaches to early intervention for young children with special needs and their families. *Young Children, 59*(5), 38–43.

Odom, S. L., & Wolery, M. (2003). A unified theory of practice in early intervention/early childhood special education: Evidence-based practices. *The Journal of Special Education, 37*(3), 164–173.

Rump, M.L. (2002). Involving fathers of young children with special needs. *Young Children, 57*(6), 18–20.

Watson, L. R., Baranek, G. T., & DiLavore, P. C. (2003). Toddlers with autism: Developmental perspectives. *Infants and Young Children, 16*(3), 201–214.

DEVELOPMENTALLY APPROPRIATE PRACTICE

NAEYC's first position statement on Developmentally Appropriate Practice (DAP) had two main motivations:

■ The process of accrediting centers required widely accepted and specific definitions of what constituted excellent practices in early childhood education.

■ A proliferation of programs had inappropriate practices and expectations for their children, largely based on premature academic learning.

The original position statement did enhance the early childhood profession, although it was not received with universal acceptance, so a revised position statement clarified some of the previous misunderstandings and expanded the vision of good practices.

Teachers should keep the principles firmly in mind when making professional decisions and use the statement in conversations with others regarding appropriate practices. Colleagues, administrators, and family members all have their individual understandings of what to do with young children. It is, therefore, useful for every teacher to have a copy of the position statement. In a conversation, you can use the position statement to replace the idea of personal opinions with the weight of the professional body of knowledge. Excerpts from the position statement (Bredekamp & Copple, 1997) are included for you to read. But, before you read the excerpts, please respond to the following questions.

1. How do you personally define the phrase *developmentally appropriate practices*?

2. How do you use your personal definition to guide your interactions/curriculum planning with very young children? Provide at least one specific example.

APPLYING GUIDELINES FOR DEVELOPMENTALLY APPROPRIATE PRACTICE

The following sections summarize some of the ways NAEYC's DAP guidelines can be implemented in your daily work with children.

- Create a Caring Environment among Children and Adults
  Children can
  - learn personal responsibility.
  - develop constructive relationships with others.
  - respect individual and cultural differences.
  Adults can
  - get to know each child, taking into account individual differences and developmental levels.
  - adjust the pace and content of the curriculum so that children can be successful most of the time.
  - bring each child's culture and language into the setting.
  - teach children to value others' differences.

- The Curriculum and Schedule Allow Children to Select and Initiate Their Own Activities
  Children can
  - learn through active involvement in a variety of learning experiences.
  - build independence by taking on increasing responsibilities.
  - initiate their own activities to follow their interests.
  Adults can
  - provide a variety of materials and activities that are concrete and real.
  - provide a variety of work places and spaces.
  - arrange the environment so that children can work alone or in groups.
  - extend children's learning by posing problems and asking thought-provoking questions.
  - add complexity to tasks as needed.
  - model, demonstrate, and provide information so children can progress in their learning.

■ The Program Is Organized and Integrated So That Children Develop a Deeper Understanding of Key Concepts and Skills
Children can
- engage in activities that reflect their current interests.
- inquire or ask questions of materials, people, and relationships.
- plan and predict outcomes of their research.
- share information and knowledge with others.

Adults can
- plan related activities and experiences that broaden children's knowledge and skills.
- design curriculum to foster important skills such as literacy and numeracy.
- build curriculum using knowledge of state and national guidelines for development and learning, when available.
- adapt instruction for children who are ahead or behind age-appropriate expectations.
- plan curriculum so that children achieve important developmental goals.

■ Activities and Experiences Help Children Develop a Positive Self-Image within a Democratic Community
Children can
- learn through reading books about other cultures.
- read about current events and discuss how these relate to different cultures.
- value differences among their peers, including children with disabilities.

Adults can
- provide culturally and nonsexist activities and materials that foster children's self-identity.
- design the learning environment so children can learn new skills while using their native language.
- allow children to demonstrate their learning using their own language.

■ Activities and Experiences Develop Children's Awareness of the Importance of Community Involvement
Children
- are ready and eager to learn about the world outside their immediate environment.
- are open to considering different ways of thinking or doing things.

- can benefit from contact with others outside their homes or child care setting.

Adults

- encourage awareness of the community at large.
- plan experiences in facilities within the community.
- bring outside resources and volunteers into the child care setting.
- encourage children to plan their involvement based on their own interests.

Now that you have read key aspects of the Guidelines for Developmentally Appropriate Practice, please answer the following reflective questions.

1. List things that you learned, were surprised by, or reinforced prior beliefs while reading the information from the position statement.

   a. Learned:

   b. Surprised:

   c. Reinforced:

2. Without looking back at your previous answer, how would you define the phrase *developmentally appropriate practices* now?

3. How does your second definition of DAP (in question 2) differ from the one you wrote *before* reading the position statement? In what ways are the changes related to your responses in question 1?

As you may have noticed while reading the summary of the position statement, creating a caring community is an important component of DAP. Implied in the position statement, but never stated directly, is the need for adults, teachers, and family members to respect young children. Although this may seem obvious, it is often unclear what that would look when interacting with very young children, that is, infants and toddlers. Hence, an article, "Respecting Infants and Toddlers: Strategies for Best Practice," has been included. Before reading the article, respond to the following reflective questions:

1. Think about the last time someone demonstrated respect to you. What behaviors did they display? How did you feel?

2. Make a list of behaviors that you find to be disrespectful. Ask a colleague to do the same. Compare the two lists. What did you learn about respectful and disrespectful behaviors?

RESPECTING INFANTS & TODDLERS: STRATEGIES FOR BEST PRACTICE

BY TERRI JO SWIM, Ph.D.

Respect. What does this term mean for infant and toddler teachers? Can or should this word be used to describe teachers' behaviors when interacting with very young children? Before such questions can be answered, a definition of respect must be established. Use the following prompts to assist with thinking about your definition of respect.

Stop and Ponder: Take a moment to write down your personal definition of respect.

(1) Circle the features that are vital to your definition (i.e., these aspects could not be removed without greatly altering your definition), and (2) Identify features that seem less important to your definition. Cross them out. What remains? Review your new definition. Does it more succinctly reflect your beliefs?

Now, compare your definition with the one found in the *American Heritage*® Dictionary of the English Language (2000):

- To feel or show differential regard for

- To avoid violation of or interference with

- The state of being regarded with honor or esteem

- Willingness to show consideration or appreciation

Although the dictionary definition may initially seem clear-cut, its application to teachers of infants and toddlers is not immediately apparent. Is it respectful, for example, for a teacher to pick up an infant without preparing the child for the move? Is it respectful of a toddler to encourage her to make decisions? Is it respectful of an infant teacher to secure interesting posters to the wall for the children to look at? Is it respectful of a teacher to teach toddlers how to interact with one another? Your definition, more than likely, already connects closely to your behavior. This article will present examples of how we can translate the formal definition of respect into useful examples of behaviors with young children.

Demonstrating Respect

If we declare respect an educational value (Rinaldi, 2001), then we need to consider both personal and professional basis for this decision. As an individual, your beliefs are impacted by current and past experiences, such as how you are regarded by your supervisor or coworkers and how you were treated in your family of origin or in educational settings. Both positive and negative experiences give shape and form to your belief system. The early childhood profession clearly desires to minimize negative influences and maximize positive ones. Hence, guidelines for best practice clearly articulate respect as the basis for appropriate interactions with very young children and families (Bredekamp & Copple, 1997; Gonzalez-Mena & Eyer, 2001; Herr & Swim, 2002; Lally et al., 1995; NAEYC, 1998; Swim and Muza, 1999). Demonstrating respect is not just about feeling good; for young children, it is about adults acting intentionally to promote optimal development and learning. As Herr and Swim (2003) state. "Respect must be demonstrated in your behaviors. More importantly, respect for infants and toddlers must be something that emanates from inside of you. You have to believe that infants and toddlers are worthy of your time and attention as individuals, because a respectful relationship is vital to all aspects of child development" (p. 9).

As individuals and as a profession, our understanding of respect has been expanded by the work and writing of educators in Reggio Emilia, Italy (see, for example, Edwards, Gandini, & Foreman, 1998). They believe that children must be viewed as having rights, rather than simply needs (Ghedini, 2001; Malaguzzi, 1993; Rinaldi, 1998). If we concur that one of our basic human rights is to be respected and treated in a respectful manner, then we have to begin at birth building a strong foundation for the development of respect. What better way to teach respect than to intentionally demonstrate it during your work (e.g., when planning environments and experiences or when interacting) with young children?

Let's take two components of the definition of respect provided earlier and present specific examples with very young children. These examples will illustrate how to apply the abstract definition of respect to our work with infants and toddlers.

To Avoid Interfering, Allow Time

When adults allow time for children to try and/or to complete a task before providing assistance or necessary intervention, they are demonstrating respect. Infants and toddlers are reveling in their newly acquired skills. However, mastery only comes with repeated opportunities for practice. In addition to providing time for mastery, teachers must purposely monitor the type and degree of support provided. In order to know how best to respond, adults must be intimately familiar with the needs, interests, and abilities of the infants and toddlers in their care (Bredekamp & Copple, 1997; Lally et al., 1995; Swim & Muza, 1999). For some children, it may be sufficient to provide a verbal explanation or question while other children may require physical assistance. Watch, however, that you do not rely on one approach too much. All children need a balance of responses so that they can perfect skills and view themselves as capable.

Consider this scene:

A toddler walks out of the bathroom with water dripping from his hands. The teacher asks the toddler, "Did you get your hands dried?" The toddler stops and looks at his hands. He shakes his head "no." The teacher asks, "Do you need me to get you another paper towel or can you get it yourself?" The toddler smiles at her and returns to the bathroom.

Encourage Children to Make Choices

Another way to think about "refraining from or interfering with" is to allow young children to make choices or decisions. This aspect includes not only the explicit choices you provide throughout a day, but also the choices children make independently. Children, especially toddlers, need to be provided choices to help them feel in control of their environment (Marion, 2003).

COMPETENCIES FOR INFANT-TODDLER ARTICLE

The Child Development Associates (CDA) competencies that can be used for this article are:

- To establish and maintain a safe, healthy learning environment

- To ensure a well-run, purposeful program responsive to participant needs

For more information on the CDA competency requirements, contact the Council for Early Childhood Recognition at (800) 424-4310.

This article helps meet the following Certified Childcare Professionals (CCP) professional ability areas:

- The ability to establish and maintain a safe, healthy, and nurturing learning environment

- The ability to establish and maintain a well-run and purposeful early childhood educational environment for children

For more information on the CCP certification, contact the National Child Care Association at (800) 543-7161.

Additionally, when you accept an idea that a toddler has generated independently you are sending the message that she has worthy ideas.

Consider this scene:

Jacki, a family child care provider, is caring for five children on a warm, but drizzly, summer afternoon. One child is asleep, one is upset so Jacki is walking with her, and the other three are engaged in quiet activities. Miranda, a toddler, is looking out the window and decides she wants to go outside and "stomp in puddle." Jacki considers the mess it might make, but then remembers the fun she had jumping in puddles. She considers the potential hazards (e.g., lightning) and sets some clear limits for Miranda's behavior. Miranda races outside, jumps in the first puddle she comes to, and turns to look back at Jacki in the window, clearly proud that she made such a good decision to go outside!

Value Individual Styles

We can also demonstrate respect by valuing individual children's ways of doing and being. Not all children are vivacious and outgoing, for example. Some children like to observe from a distance before joining others in play. Letting them observe and join in the play when they are ready shows that you respect their style of initiating interactions. Moreover, children, like adults, have special routines or unique ways of doing things. Close observation and documentation on your part coupled with frequent, open communication with families will help you to understand each child's unique characteristics and know how to respond respectfully to these characteristics.

Consider this scene:

Hector and Miguel are two children in a mixed-age classroom in a full-day child care program. They are both on the rug building independent structures with unit blocks. Simone crawls over to the edge of the carpet and watches them. She touches a block and babbles. Juan, the teacher, says, "You are watching them build." Simone looks at him, babbles again, and begins to crawl toward the mirror hanging on the wall.

"To Regard with Honor or Esteem," Create Meaningful Environments

We show children that they are worthy as individuals and deserving of high regard when we create environments and experiences that are meaningful. A key component of best practices is providing age-appropriate, individual, and culturally appropriate experiences that have intellectual integrity (Bredekamp & Copple, 1997). In other words, the children are engaged in experiences that are relevant to their lives and lead to greater understanding of the world and their places in it. One way to deepen understanding is to engage in ongoing investigations with young children (Hehn & Beneke, 2003; Helm & Katz, 2001; Katz & Chard, 1989). Projects to help the children "see the extraordinary in the ordinary" (Gandini, January 27, 2001, personal communication) are particularly engaging for older toddlers. In other words, you do not have to create projects on "novel" topics. Listen to the children with your eyes and ears. What are they doing? What interests them? What do they babble or talk about? Use this information to plan experiences and investigations that support and enhance all areas of development.

Consider this scene with infants:

Tanya cares for two infants in her home. She has created special spots for them to gather and talk about families. Although they are different ages, Diego and Nerida are both experiencing separation anxiety. They are visibly distressed when their family members leave and take several minutes to calm down. Tanya laminated and displayed at the children's eye level several pictures of both children's family members so that she could converse with the infants throughout the day about those they miss. She also uses those photographs to talk about similarities and differences between Diego's and Nerida's families.

Consider this scene with toddlers:

Josy notices that Maya and Peter want to help when she sweeps the floor after lunch. She wonders if they would be interested in investigating brooms. She places a variety of brooms with different functions around the inside and outside environments. For example, she places a feather duster in the dramatic play area that is set up as a home. Beside the sensory table filled with dirt, she places a dust broom and pan. Outside, she leaves a push broom next to the building that is adjacent to the tricycle path.

Before the children arrive, she hypothesizes about how the children will use the brooms and questions she can ask. She predicts that the children will notice the differences among the brooms and so she will ask questions about how the design (e.g., shape, size) of the broom influences its function. She is also interested in provoking thinking about how two children can use one broom at the same time. Maybe later in the week or next week they can consider how to modify a broom for two people. Josy considers different ways to have the children communicate their understanding about brooms and, therefore, has available pencils; me, felt-tipped pens; white paper; and clay.

Teach Interaction Skills

Young children are inherently social. They interact with others long before they are verbal or can physically move to be in close proximity to others. Infants possess many strategies such as cooing or smiling for getting others to attend to them. Even with this high level of social interest and strategies for gaining attention, infants and toddlers lack other necessary skills (e.g., perspective-taking, problem-solving, and emotional regulation) to be successful when interacting with each other. Responsible adults perform most of an infant's or toddler's ego functions (e.g., reminding the child about appropriate behavior), thereby regulating the young child's social interactions for her (Marion, 2003). Thus, these adults do not expect very young children to be able to interact successfully with others. They realistically anticipate devoting significant amounts of time each day to helping children interact with one another and employ several strategies for this purpose. To illustrate, adults can read the nonverbal communication cues for children, describe appropriate behavior, and then allow time for interaction while maintaining close supervision.

Consider this scene:

Three infants are sitting in bouncy seats in a carpeted area. While positioning the seats so that all of the infants can see one another, the adult comments that, "It's time to talk to our friends." Skye begins to babble and looks at the adult. The adult says, "Yes, you are excited to see Rashid. He wasn't here yesterday." The adult leaves, providing time and space for the infants to interact with one another.

Listen to the Children

We communicate respect for young children when we listen to their ideas, feelings, and dreams. Listening to children who possess language is considerably easier than listening to pre-verbal children. Yet, as caregivers of infants and toddlers, we have to engage in the struggle to decide, "What is she trying to communicate with crying?" or "What does he want when he points toward the door?"

When we listen to the children and respond accordingly, it communicates that they and their ideas are important. Utilizing their ideas when planning curriculum not only recognizes the different potential of each child, but also reflects guidelines for developmentally appropriate practices. This also supports the notion that "All children have the potential, albeit in different ways, to learn and to develop their own ideas, theories, and strategies. All children also have the right to be supported in these endeavors by adults. Teachers and parents, therefore, should observe and listen to them" (Gandini & Goldhaber, 2001, p. 125).

Consider this scene:

Evelyn is standing at the "Bye, Bye Window" (Herr & Swim, 2003) watching her grandfather walk away from the building. Her fists are clenched and tears are streaming down her cheeks. The adult sits quietly beside her before saying, "You are mad that Granddad left. You wanted to leave with him." Evelyn leans against the adult and continues to cry. The adult comforts her by stating, "Granddad was sad to leave you also. He had fun playing peek-a-boo with you. But, Granddad has to go to work. He'll be back after afternoon snack."

Conclusion

Now that several examples of respectful interactions have been provided, it is time to take a moment to reflect on your interactions with young children.

Stop and Ponder: How do you show respect to the infants and toddlers in your care? What behaviors support your beliefs? What behaviors conflict with your beliefs? Say, for a moment, that a parent was observing your work with young children. How would she know that you respect young children?

It may, at first, seem hard to demonstrate respect to infants and toddlers because we are unaccustomed to thinking about very young children in this manner. In fact, it may seem easier to demonstrate respect to infants rather than toddlers. Toddlers are experiencing a developmental "tug of war" between the desire to do tasks independently and the necessity to depend on others to meet their needs. This milestone places significant stress on toddlers and adults. However, we cannot lose sight of the fact that respect is a key component in best practices and for meeting the developmental needs of infants and toddlers. This article, hopefully, has provided concrete examples of how to apply the abstract definition of respect when working with infants and toddlers.

Terri Jo Swim, Ph.D., is an Assistant Professor of early childhood education and child development at Indiana University Purdue University Fort Wayne (IPFW) in Fort Wayne, IN. She teaches undergraduate and graduate programs. Her research interests include infant-toddler and preschool curriculum, Reggio Emilia, and teacher education. This article is based on a keynote presentation from February 8, 2003, at the Infant-Toddler Institute sponsored by the Akron Area Association for the Education of Young Children.

References

American Heritage® *Dictionary of the English Language.* (2000, 4th ed.). Houghton Mifflin Company. Accessed at http://www.your dictionary.com/ahd/r/r0180400.htm on February 26, 2003.

Edwards, C., Gandini, L., & Forman, G., (Eds.). (1998). *The hundred languages of children: The Reggio Emilia approach—Advance reflections.* (2nd ed.). Westport, CT: Ablex Publishing.

Gandini, L., & Goldhaber, J. (2001). Two reflections about documentation. In L. Gandini & C. Pope Edwards, *Bambini: The Italian approach to infant/toddler care.* New York: Teachers College Press.

Ghedini, P. (2001). Change in Italian national policy for children 0–3 years old and their families: Advocacy and responsibility. In L. Gandini & C. Pope Edwards, *Bambini: The Italian approach to infant/toddler care.* New York: Teachers College Press.

Gonzalez-Mena, J., & Eyer, D. W (2001). *Infants, toddlers, and caregivers.* (5th ed.). Mountain View, CA: Mayfield Publishing Company.

Helm, J. H., & Beneke, S. (2003). *The power of projects: Meeting contemporary challenges in early childhood classrooms—Strategies and Solutions.* New York: Teachers College Press.

Helm, J. H., & Katz, L. (2001). *Young investigators: The project approach in the early years.* New York: Teachers College Press.

Herr, J., & Swim, T. (2003). *Sorting shapes, show me, and many other activities for toddlers: Creative resources infant and toddler series.* New York: Thomson Delmar Learning.

Herr, J., & Swim, T. (2002). *Creative resources for infants and toddlers.* (2nd ed.). New York: Thomson Delmar Learning.

Katz, L., & Chard, S. (1989). *Engaging children's minds: The project approach.* Greenwich, CT: Ablex Publishing Corporation.

Lally, J. R., Griffin, A., Fenichel, E., Segal, M., Szanton, E. S., & Weissbourd, B. (1995). *Caring for infants and toddlers in groups: Developmentally appropriate practices.* Washington, DC: Zero to Three.

Malaguzzi, L. (1998). History, ideas, and basic philosophy: An interview with Lella Gandini. In C. Edwards, L. Gandini, & G. Foreman (Eds.), *The hundred languages of children: The Reggio Emilia approach—Advanced reflections.* (2nd ed.). Westport, CT: Ablex Publishing, 49–98.

Malaguzzi, L. (1993). A *charter of rights.* Reggio Emilia, Italy.

Marion, M. (2003). *Guidance of young children.* (6th ed.). Upper Saddle River, NJ: Merrill.

NAEYC. (1998). Code of ethical conduct: A NAEYC Position Statement. Washington, DC: author.

Rinaldi, C. (2001). Infant-toddler centers and preschools as places of culture. In Project Zero and Reggio Children, *Making learning visible: Children as individual and group learners.* Italy: Reggio Children srl.

Rinaldi, C. (1998). Projected curriculum constructed through documentation—Progettazione: An interview with Lella Gandini. In C. Edwards, L. Gandini, & G. Foreman (Eds., *The hundred languages of children: The Reggio Emilia approach—Advanced reflections.* (2nd ed.). Westport, CT: Ablex Publishing, 113–126.

Swim, T. J., & Muza, R. (1999). Planning curriculum for infants. *Texas Child Care,* 22(4), 2–7.

Reprinted by permission. Swim, T. J. (2003, October). Respecting infants and toddlers: Strategies for best practice. *Earlychildhood NEWS,* pp. 16–17, 20–23.

Stop and Ponder . . .

After reading this article, use this space to respond to the "Stop and Ponder" questions:

1. How do you show respect to the infants and toddlers in your care? (Provide specific examples.)

2. What behaviors support your beliefs? What behaviors conflict with your beliefs?

3. Say, for a moment, that a parent was observing your work with young children. How would she know that you respect young children?

DEVELOPMENTALLY APPROPRIATE OR NOT? THAT IS THE QUESTION

Deciding whether an experience is developmentally appropriate or not is a complicated conclusion to reach. It takes much time, reflection, and, often, rereading of the guidelines. An experience designed for one toddler might be inappropriate for the entire group of toddlers. Likewise, an experience that is appropriate for a particular age group of children might be inappropriate for a particular child within the group. This section provides you with three scenarios describing classroom events. After reading the information for each scenario, decide whether you think the experience is developmentally appropriate. If you feel that you do not have enough information, write in other information that you considered when making your decision. Justify (e.g., provide reasons for) your answer by referring back to the position statement. Set aside some time to discuss these scenarios and your responses with a colleague.

Scenario 1:

Umberto is a toddler in a family child care program. He is one of two children for whom the provider partners with Early Head Start to provide services. The provider, Linda Lou, has noticed that Umberto does not like to get his hands dirty. He rarely plays with sand or paints. She decides to plan a dry sensory experience in the water table. She fills the bottom of the toddler-size sensory table with beans and rice and puts in water wheels, spoons, and measuring cups.

Other information considered:

Do you think this experience is developmentally appropriate? Provide a justification for your answer.

Scenario 2:

Suzy, a teacher for a group of infants, has read about the importance of outside play for very young children. She knows that they should get fresh air each day, weather permitting, to remain healthy. It snowed last night, and about 3 inches of new snow is on the ground. Because the temperature and wind chill are above 32°, she plans to take out all of the infants for 15 minutes today during the sunniest part of the morning. She and her co-teacher will bundle them up as quickly as possible, and she will be in charge of supervising the older, more mobile children. She is going to take out the shopping carts to provide something for them to push on the sidewalk that she cleared of snow.

Other information considered:

Do you think this experience is developmentally appropriate? Provide a justification for your answer.

Scenario 3:

Ty'rel is a teacher for a toddler group in a child care center. To provide continuity of care, his program has divided the infant/toddler groups into 2 classrooms. Ty'rel works with the "older" children from about 18 months to 36 months of age. He has been carefully observing the 8 children in his room and has noticed that 2 children in particular need to practice their gross motor skills, especially balancing. Ty'rel has decided to set up a balance beam in his classroom. The top of the beam is about 5 inches high from the mats he has placed around it. He has agreed with his co-teacher that one of them will stand near the balance beam whenever a child is near it.

Other information considered:

Do you think this experience is developmentally appropriate? Provide a justification for your answer.

EMOTIONAL DEVELOPMENT, continued	OBSERVED	
25 to 36 Months	Date	Comments
Experiences increase in number of fears		
Begins to understand the consequences of basic emotions		
Learns skills for coping with strong emotions		
Seeks to communicate more feelings with specific words		
Shows signs of empathy and caring		
Loses control of emotions and throws temper tantrums		
Able to recover from temper tantrums		
Enjoys helping with chores such as cleaning up toys or carrying grocery bags		
Begins to show signs of readiness for toileting		
Desires that routines be carried out exactly as has been done in the past		

Additional Observations for Emotional Development

The developmental milestones listed are based on universal patterns of when various traits emerge. Because each child is unique, certain traits may develop at an earlier or later age.

Make a copy of the checklist for each child and place on clipboards in handy locations around the classroom. Other checklists are available or can be constructed that focus on behaviors that are most likely to be displayed in a particular area of the classroom. When you observe the children at play in each center, check off skills by placing a date in the appropriate box.

TIME AND EVENT SAMPLING

Another type of observation that a teacher should perform is a time or event sampling. These are similar in focus, but different, too. A **time sampling**, used mostly with mobile children, asks the teacher to set a timer, and each time the timer goes off the teacher looks at a particular child and writes down what the child is doing. Again only the facts are written, nothing else.

> The timer is set to go off every 10 minutes. I will look at Joshua and see what he is doing when I hear the timer. The timer goes off; I look at Joshua and note that he is stacking nesting cups on the floor in the block area. The timer goes off again, and I note that he is toddling around the dress up area holding a spoon and cup.

DEVELOPING A RESPONSIVE, EMERGENT CURRICULUM

Developing curriculum involves observing, evaluating and reflecting, planning, implementing, and reflecting further. Although this may sound complicated, it does not have to be. In fact, if you have collected observational data, you have completed the first step in creating curriculum. The next step involves reading and evaluating the data you have gathered. Set aside time daily or weekly, as your schedule permits, to read over your data and determine the abilities, strengths, and needs of each child in your room. When planning curriculum, balance experiences that are familiar and novel, are accomplished with a peer and alone, occur inside and outdoors, and are completed independently and with assistance from a teacher. Moreover, traditional content areas (e.g., literacy, mathematics, science) should be addressed through play and inquiry. Infants and toddlers, like older children, learn in an integrated manner; projects are a perfect way for building ideas and concepts over time.

Reflecting on your observational notes helps you to understand what skills the children have mastered, are working on, and are ready for. After knowing this, write your ideas of how to support and enhance their development and learning using a lesson plan form. Your early childhood program may have a set form for you to use. If such a form is not available from your program, some are included later in this section that other infant and toddler teachers have found useful. While implementing the curricular experiences, record your observations of the children. Note what the child could do alone and what she did with assistance. This creates a loop in the curriculum planning cycle. As such, when you begin to develop curriculum the next time, you have additional data from which to make instructional decisions.

To help illustrate this process, the "Planning Curriculum for Infants" article is included next. After reading the article, respond to the questions that immediately follow.

PLANNING CURRICULUM FOR INFANTS

by Terri Jo Swim and Robin Muza

Maria and Antonio are teachers in an infant classroom. They have eight children enrolled in their room, although they never have more than six infants on a given day. They follow their state's guidelines for infant care, but still do not know what to say when parents and co-workers ask what they "teach" the babies. In fact, they wonder themselves if and what they are teaching. It seems as though they spend the greatest amount of time feeding, rocking, and diapering children.

This feeling is not uncommon for infant teachers. The traditional notion of teaching seems—and is—inappropriate for infants. They won't sit in a group (if they can sit at all). They can't talk. So how do teachers recognize the needs, interests, and abilities of infants to create a curriculum that teaches them? Theories of child development and principles of developmentally appropriate practice can guide your answers to these questions.

Developmentally Appropriate Practices for Infants

Experienced teachers of infants recognize the needs, interests, and abilities of infants in their classroom (Bredekamp and Copple, 1997). Some of these needs, interests, and abilities are common for a particular age of children. Typically, infants follow a developmental pattern. For example, infants typically are able to sit without help around 7 months of age. When they are able to sit in this manner, they usually begin to creep or crawl (Berk, 1996).

Development during infancy is different than during any other period of life. Here are five reasons:

- This period of growth and development is rapid. Noticeable changes occur monthly, weekly, and, in some cases, daily.

- All areas of development are intertwined. Mental, or cognitive, development, for example, cannot be separated from physical development. Changes in one area result in changes in another area.

- This time is a foundation for later development and learning (Shore, 1997).

- Infants depend upon adults to meet all their needs.

- Infants have no effective skills for coping with discomfort and stress, so they are open to harm (Morrison, 1996).

While some needs, interests, and abilities are typical to all infants, others are specific to a particular child. These represent the unique characteristics of each child in your room (Bredekamp and Copple, 1997). Most of these differences are the child's desires or special preferences. For example, José likes to have his back rubbed before he falls asleep at naptime, while Naomi likes to hug her blanket and be alone.

Also, some needs, interests, and abilities are specific to cultures or subcultures the children experience in society and in their homes (Bredekamp and Copple, 1997). In other words, these are the beliefs and values held by each individual's family. For example, Houa lives with his father in an extended family. In this household, family needs are more important than individual needs. Therefore, you might expect that Houa' s reaction to situations, such as stress, would be different than other children's.

How Infant Development Impacts Curriculum

Curriculum is everything you do with a child day-by-day and throughout the year. According to Greenman and Stonehouse (1996), "curriculum is the framework and rationale for doing what you do, not a list of activities." If your curriculum is developmentally appropriate for infants, it will reflect both the typical features of infant development and the unique characteristics and cultures of the children in your care. Ideally, an infant curriculum will do the following:

- Emphasize relationships with people.

  The teachers assist infants in learning that they are a vital part of a relationship. For example, teachers who consistently respond to cries in a caring manner teach that communication is an important tool for getting needs met.

In this case, they are building a strong sense of trust and helping the infants to learn that they can count on others during times of stress. According to psychosocial theory (Erikson, 1950) and attachment theory (Bowlby, 1969, 1980), developing a sense of trust is one of the main developmental tasks for infants. Both theories suggest that learning to trust others affects how well children will fare socially later in life. In fact, researchers have found that infants who trust their caregivers have better relationships with peers later in life than those who don't (Cassidy et al., 1996; Park and Waters, 1978; Turner, 1991).

- Establish a safe and emotionally supportive environment.

A reliable set of routines provides a sense of security, especially those associated with pleasurable feelings (Herr and Swim, 1999). Knowing that outside play follows naptime, for example, helps infants order and predict events. However, these routines need to be flexible to ensure that individual needs are met. Meeting individual needs within a set of routines creates a comfortable environment, free from too much stress. For example, it is getting close to lunchtime and Faustina is unusually tired today. You decide to feed her first so that she can be in her crib earlier than normal. By meeting Faustina's individual needs, you are lowering her level of stress.

- Focus on learning through play.

A stimulating infant classroom allows infants to learn through their senses. The environment has safe, interesting items that infants can see, touch, taste, hear, and smell (Piaget, 1952). True exploration requires that infants be free to move their bodies. Laying them on blankets indoors and outdoors, propping them up with pillows (after creating a safe fall zone for them), and urging them to crawl across the floor are all ways to support their learning. Infants do not learn a new concept or skill by engaging in an experience one time. They need lots of repetition. They are just as interested in the 50th reading of *Good Night Moon* (Brown, 1947) as they were in the first! Infants also need the opportunity to learn new skills independently through trial and error. Sometimes, there is no better way for them to figure out something new than to start with something that does not work.

- Encourage learning through social interactions.

  Infants, like older children, do not learn in a vacuum. They learn by watching others and imitating what they see. They also learn by interacting with others. Infants need the chance to interact with toddlers, but with close supervision to prevent accidents. Although infants are not skilled at interacting with each other, they can benefit from observing. For example, propping up Bradley so that he can see Carmen while playing provides each child with an example of how to explore toys. Infants also need the chance to interact with older children and adults.

- Help infants meet developmental milestones in all areas of development.

  An ideal curriculum addresses all developmental areas—physical, self-help, cognitive, language, social, and emotional. It considers the whole child; it does not over-emphasize one area and ignore another. For example, Natasha's learning to separate from Mom is just as important as her learning to creep, crawl, and walk or to find toys hidden from sight. However, because children develop at their own individual rates, teachers may need to spend a little extra time with a child on one area or another.

Assessment of Infants

A teacher learns about an infant's needs, interests, and abilities through assessment. This means that you observe, record, and evaluate a child's behavior so you can make decisions about that child's developmental needs (Herr and Swim, 1999).

Assessments, like curriculum activities, need to be developmentally appropriate (Bredekamp and Rosegrant, 1995). This kind of assessment has the following characteristics:

- It is designed to gather information about all areas of development for each infant.

- It focuses on understanding and valuing infants for their current level of development. In other words, the goal is to recognize each child's strengths.

- It results in benefits to the child. For example, you observe that Carrie sleeps fitfully near the window, so you move her crib to a quiet corner.

- It reflects the ages and experiences of the children in care. At the same time, it recognizes individual variations in learners and allows for differences in styles and rates of learning. For example, when doing a language assessment, you take into account the fact that Yuji speaks Japanese at home and English in child care.

- It happens regularly. Teachers observe each child in a wide variety of situations—while being fed, resting, playing outside, having a diaper changed. Therefore, assessments are embedded into the curriculum and integrated into the daily routine. In this way, evaluations of the children's behavior take place in a natural setting.

- It involves parents. Teachers communicate with parents or other family members through conversation and written notes about each child's experiences at home and in the classroom. Teachers use this information in evaluating a child's development.

How Assessments Impact Curriculum

What teachers learn about children through assessments helps determine what will be in the curriculum. Ideally, you will plan a balance of activities that support, enhance, and foster all areas of development (Herr and Swim, 1999). Some experiences will be repetitious and represent developmental tasks the child has accomplished. Some experiences will provide opportunities to master developmental tasks the infant is working on. Other experiences will challenge and extend the child's development by requiring a slightly higher skill level. This last experience works much like scaffolding, connecting the known with the unknown. As infants struggle at this higher level, they may need more support and help from adults to build their confidence as competent learners.

What does curriculum development look like in real life? Here's an example to illustrate.

Maria and Antonio, the teachers mentioned earlier, have assessed their infants during routine care times such as feeding, diapering, and the transition to naptime. They have begun to notice several things. In feeding, Jose and Sophia are just beginning to put their hands around the bottle to help hold it. Naomi and Zachary hold on to their bottles well, and they are also beginning to show interest in holding spoons. Meanwhile, Faustina and Houa feed themselves finger foods and are improving each day in their use of spoons.

As a result of their assessments, Maria and Antonio have decided to make some changes when feeding the infants during the upcoming week. With José and Sophia, they will encourage each child to hold the bottle independently. With Naomi and Zachary, they will continue to invite each child to hold the bottle independently. In addition, they will give each child a spoon to hold while being fed and say something like, "This is a spoon. You can use it to eat your cereal." With Faustina and Houa, Maria and Antonio plan to cut the finger foods into smaller pieces to really work the small muscles of the thumb and forefinger. They will also continue suggesting that these two infants feed themselves using a spoon.

How to Communicate with Others about Your Curriculum

You have observed, recorded, evaluated, and implemented a curriculum that reflects the individual needs, interests, and abilities of the infants in your room. But your job as a teacher is not finished. You still need to communicate with others about what you are doing and why. You can accomplish this in several ways:

- Display information about development on a bulletin board.

- When talking with parents or guardians at the beginning or end of the day, share things you have noticed about their individual child.

- Hold regular parent-teacher conferences to discuss the developmental progress of their child.

- Share information with parents.

- Provide weekly newsletters to tell parents about experiences that you have planned or implemented to promote learning and development in your classroom. When appropriate, you can suggest ways to adapt those experiences at home.

What do infant teachers teach? They teach the beginning skills that are the building blocks for later development and learning. They teach these skills in their daily interactions with infants and families and in the curriculum they create for the children: By paying careful attention to the needs, interests, and abilities of the children in their care, infant teachers can and do foster development and learning.

References

Berk, L. E. *Infants, Children, and Adolescents,* 2nd ed. Boston: Allyn and Bacon, 1996.

Bowlby, J. *Attachment and Loss: Vol. 1.* New York: Basic Books, 1969.

Bowlby, J. *Attachment and Loss: Vol. 3.* New York: Basic Books, 1980.

Bredekamp, S. and C. Copple, eds. *Developmentally Appropriate Practice in Early Childhood Programs,* Rev. ed. Washington, D.C.: National Association for the Education of Young Children, 1997.

Bredekamp, S. and T. Rosegrant, eds. *Reaching Potentials: Transforming Early Childhood Curriculum and Assessment, Vol. 2.* Washington, D.C.: National Association for the Education of Young Children, 1995.

Brown, M. W. *Goodnight Moon.* New York: HarperCollins Publishers, 1947.

Cassidy, J.; K. L. Scolton; S. J. Kirsh; and R. D. Parke. "Attachment and representations of peer relationships," *Developmental Psychology* (1996) 32, 892–904.

Erikson, E. H. *Childhood and Society.* New York: Norton, 1950.

Greenman, J. and A. Stonehouse, *Prime Times: A Handbook for Excellence in Infant and Toddler Programs.* St. Paul, Minn.: Redleaf Press, 1996.

Herr, J. and T. J. Swim. *Creative Resources for Infants and Toddlers.* Clifton Park, N.Y.: Thomson Delmar Learning, 1999.

Morrison, G. S. *Early Childhood Education Today.* Upper Saddle River, N.J.: Merrill, 1996.

Park, K. A. and E. Waters. "Security of attachment and preschool friendships," *Child Development* (1978) 60, 1076–1081.

Piaget, J. *The Origins of Intelligence in Children.* New York: International Universities Press, 1952.

Shore, R. *Rethinking the Brain: New Insights into Early Development.* New York: Families and Work Institute, 1997.

Turner, P. J. "Relations between attachment, gender, and behavior with peers in preschool," *Child Development* (1991) 62, 1475–1489.

About the Authors

Terri Jo Swim, Ph.D., and Robin Muza, M.S., teach early childhood education and child development courses at the University of Wisconsin–Stout in Menomonie, Wisconsin Together, they have presented at local and regional conferences. As a graduate student, Terri was a master teacher at The University of Texas at Austin Child and Family Laboratory School. Robin has had more than 15 years of experience with young children and parents, including having operated her own family child care business.

Reprinted by permission. Swim, T. J. & Muza, R. (1999, Spring). Planning curriculum for infants. *Texas Child Care, The Quarterly Journal for Caregivers Everywhere*, pp. 2–7.

Questions

After reading both curriculum articles, respond to the following questions:

1. What does good curriculum for infants and toddlers look like in a classroom setting? Connect at least three points from the article in your response.

2. Assume for a moment that your program desires to create an outdoor learning environment for infants and toddlers. How would you create partnerships with family and community members to plan, design, and use the space?

The following Block Plan form is used by teachers who just recently began working with a new group of infants. They have 6 children in their room ranging in age from 4 to 8 months. To best address the rapid developmental changes during this time period, they plan curricular experiences on a daily basis. Each day at nap time, they decide what experiences to provide on the next day. Notice that the form has space for listing experiences for the group and individual children.

Sample Block Plan for Infants		
Today is: November 12		Teachers are: Ramona and Alice
Group Experiences	Individual Child Experiences	Observation Notes for child
Greeting:	Norma:	(Obs Notes for Norma)
"Good morning, ___" song	Peek-a-boo with bear	
Tummy Time/Floor Experiences:	Zachary:	

(continued)

Sample Block Plan for Infants, continued

Pillow case with objects to pull out while lying on belly	Hold spoon while eating cereal	
Language/Communication:	LaTisha	
• Chant nursery rhymes	Tummy time: Pillow and mirror to prop on belly and look at self	
• Repeat children's vocalizations (e.g., coos, babble)		
Rattles/Manipulatives:	Katia	
• Put staking toys and lids for clapping out for those who can sit upright	Have push toy available, since already taking steps	
• Activity gym with objects for reaching/grabbing		
Physical:	Byron	
Wind chime stretch outside	Read board books *with* him to engage vocalization	
Routine Care:	Sheryll	
Help hold bottle while eating	Talk about anger at dad leaving (separation anxiety)	
Count toes during diapering		

Sample Lesson Plan Form

Teacher: Kathleen

Age/Group: Mixed-Age Toddlers

Experience/Activity Title: Mystery Footprints

Observation/Assessment:

Bria, Damon, and Radi walked around the stepping stones at the perimeter of the outside learning environment. They had to take huge steps to stay on the stones. They laughed as they jumped from one stone to another. When Bria fell "off," Damon said "go again." She joined back in the game.

Materials/Preparation:

Scissors, construction paper, baby powder

Cut shape of footprint in construction paper. Place cut-out of footprint over carpet and sprinkle baby powder to make shape. Do several as if person walked through room with dirty feet.

CAUTION: Be sure to keep powder away from tile or vinyl flooring because it could make the floor slippery.

Sample Lesson Plan Form, continued

Procedures—Introduction:

Observe the children's reactions to the footprints. Ask them questions such as, "What could those be?" "How did they get there?" "Where do you think they lead?"

Steps for conducting experience:

Suggest that the children follow the footprints around the room to see where they lead.

Discuss how they are walking on the footprints by saying, for example, "You are stepping on each footprint. Left, right, left, right." Or "You just jumped from one footprint to the other."

Guidance Considerations:

Assist toddlers with sharing the space. To illustrate, say, "One person per footprint. Bria is going first. Then, Derek. Now, it is your turn, Radi."

Discuss how it is hard to wait for a turn. "Waiting is hard. Everyone wants to walk on the footprints, so we have to share. You are waiting for your turn."

Strategies for Guiding Learning:

After the children have had time to investigate the footprints, promote inquiry by asking again about where they came from and where they are going. Encourage the children to brainstorm and avoid discouraging any answer.

Ask, "Have you ever left a footprint on the floor? Tell us more."

Closure:

"You spent ___ minutes walking on the footprints. Together we had many different ideas about the footprints."

Transition to next event:

"Let's all hop to the bathroom to wash our hands before snack."

Open-ended/Inquiry Questions to ask:	
Where did the footprints come from?	
Where do the footprints lead?	
Adaptations for lesson:	Extensions for lesson:
Invite Jonathon to walk first because he is easily distracted.	Encourage children to find other ways to get from one footprint to another (hop, crawl, slither on belly).
Give Leilani the choice of using her wheelchair or walker to follow the footprints.	
Observational Notes:	

Experience adapted from Herr, J., & Swim, T. (2002). *Creative resources for infants and toddlers.* (2nd ed.). Clifton Park, NY: Thomson Delmar Learning, p. 269.

After investing much time and effort in creating curricular experiences, sometimes things do not go as planned. You intended to spend the first predicted nice day of summer in the outdoor learning environment, and there is an unexpected rainstorm. What will you do? It is your day off, and you get a call at the last minute to cover for a coworker who is ill. You cannot find his lesson plans. What activities can you implement with his group of toddlers? You were promised that the materials you needed for your planned art activity would be on site when you arrived at work, but there was a shipping delay, and they aren't there. What is an alternative activity you can set up and implement? Being prepared at all times with a few back-up activities that are appropriate for the age of children with whom you work will make your job much less stressful.

This is where curriculum planning books can be very useful. Herr and Swim (2002), in their book *Creative Resources for Infants and Toddlers* (2nd ed.), for example, provide more than 300 specially designed activities for infants and toddlers. All of these experiences are grounded in knowledge of developmental milestones and arranged according to age and developmental area. Thus, one can quickly and easily select activities that correspond to the needs of the children.

In addition, a number of Web sites offer sample lesson plans for teachers. Select lesson plans carefully to meet the pre-identified needs of the children in your group. In other words, search the Web looking for an experience to promote fine motor skills for a child with sensory impairment. This will prevent you for getting sidetracked by "cute" or "fun-looking" activities. Be continually aware that the Web is a tool for meeting your goal of gathering ideas for meeting the needs of the children in your classroom. When downloading lesson plans from the Internet or another source, be sure to carefully examine each plan to insure that it meets the developmental needs of the child or group of children. Also make sure that all plans include the following:

- Area of development addressed
- Age group that activity is intended for
- Materials needed
- Directions for the activity

The following provides a list of additional resources about curriculum development for infants and toddlers, but do not forget to check the resources section of this manual for a list of Web sites with lesson plans and other free materials for teachers.

- Bredekamp, S., & Copple, C. (1997). (Eds.). *Developmentally appropriate practice in early childhood programs. Revised edition.* Washington, DC: NAEYC. Also available on the Web at http://www.naeyc.org. On the home page, do a search for Positions and then click on Position Statements.

- Geist, E. (2003). Infants and toddlers exploring mathematics. *Young Children, 58*(1), 10–12.

- Freeman, R., & Swim, T. J. (2003). A critical reflection on using food as learning materials. *Journal of Early Childhood Teacher Education, 24,* 83–88.

- NAEYC (2004). http://www.journal.naeyc.org. On the home page, do a search for Arts Education Partnership and then click on Developmental Benchmark's and Stages for a list of developmental characteristics of children from birth to age eight with accompanying art experiences.

- Rofrano, F. (2002). "I care for you": A reflection on caring as infant curriculum. *Young Children, 57*(1), 49–51.

- Szanton, E. S. (2001). Viewpoint. For America's infants and toddlers, are important values threatened by our zeal to "teach"? *Young Children, 56*(1), 15–21.

- Torquati, J., & Barber, J. (2005). Dancing with trees: Infants and toddlers in the garden. *Young Children, 60*(3), 40–46.

- Wein, C. A., Stacey, S., Keating, B-L. H., Rowlings, J. D., & Cameron, H. (2002). The doll project: Handmade dolls as a framework for emergent curriculum. *Young Children, 57*(1), 33–38.

BOOKS FOR CHILDREN

Reading aloud is a wonderful gift you can give to children. Through sharing an interesting book, you introduce children to a world they might not otherwise be able to visit. Through books, you can travel anywhere you like, have experiences outside the realm of your current environment, participate in wonderful fantasies; and be saddened and then uplifted.

Children's desire to read and the ability to do so is fostered by reading to them as soon as they are born. Even babies can enjoy looking at picture books and hearing simple stories. Preschoolers love to have favorite books read to them repeatedly. As children move into the school years, they can sustain their interest in longer books that are divided into chapters. When they realize the joy that comes from good books, they are more motivated to read on their own.

Many textbooks provide suggestions for setting up reading corners and providing books for children to read by themselves. This section will focus on books that you can read aloud to infants and toddlers individually or in small groups. Remember that the more you read, the better you will become at doing so. When the books have been enjoyed in a group setting, add them to the book corner for children to read alone. In addition, teachers often create lending arrangements, where children can take home books for their parents to read and then return. Teachers who believe in the importance of reading choose the best of children's literature and involve families in reading.

HOW TO GET CHILDREN TO LISTEN AND WANT MORE

- Schedule several times each day for reading. Times might include after arrival, when relaxing before nap, when waking up after nap, or toward the end of the day when children are tired. Also be sure to respond to a child's indication that she wants to read. Make sure the setting is comfortable.

- Choose books that you also enjoy, perhaps one you read as a child. Preview the book before presenting it to the children. You may find passages that you will want to shorten.

- The first time you read a book, state the title and author. Research some interesting facts about the author and share them with the children. If there is an illustrator, include that information as well.

- When reading to a small group, sit among the children in a more intimate placement. This will draw them to you and the book and help associate positive emotions with reading.

- Occasionally stop and ask, "What do you think is going to happen next?" Do not expect that the infants and some toddlers will respond verbally. However, this is one way to get children thinking and thus promote cognitive development.

- Read at a pace that will allow children to build mental images of the characters or setting. Change your pace to coincide with the action of the story. Slow your pace and lower you voice during a suspenseful spot. Speed it up a little when the action is moving quickly.

- Allow time for discussion only if children want to do so. Let them voice fears, ask questions, or share their thoughts about the book. Follow the children's lead and avoid turning it into a quiz.

- Practice reading aloud, trying to vary your expression or your tone of voice.

THINGS TO AVOID

- Don't read a book that you do not enjoy; your feelings will be sensed by the children.

- Stop reading a book when it becomes obvious that it was a poor choice. If you preview the book before presenting it to the children, you may avoid this kind of mistake. However, infants' and toddlers' moods vary and on some days they will be more receptive to reading than on other days.

- Do not be fooled by awards. Just because a book has received a national book award does not mean that it is suitable for your particular group of children or individual children within your group.

- Don't impose your own interpretations or reactions to the story on the children. Let them express their own understanding and feelings.

The following pages contain a list of board books that can easily be used with infants and toddlers. This list of books published since 2000 has been arranged according to topical areas. Do not hesitate to read picture books designed for preschool children when a toddler or group of toddlers demonstrates that they are ready for a storyline or more content.

ALPHABET/SPELLING

Hallinan, P. K. *A, B, C, I Love You.* CandyCane Press, 2002.

Higham, Jon Atlas. *Spelling Three-Letter Words.* Buster Books, 2003.

Inches, Alison & Winfield, Alison (Illustrator). *An ABC Adventure: a Lift-the-Flap Alphabet Book.* Little Simon, 2003.

Katz, Karen. *What does Baby Say?: a Lift-the-Flap Book.* Little Simon, 2003.

Marzollo, Jean & Wick, Walter (Illustrator). *I Spy Little Letters.* Scholastic, 2000.

Parett, Lisa. *Princess A B C.* Sterling Publishing Company, Inc., 2004.

St. Martin's Press. *First Words.* 2004.

ANIMALS—DOMESTIC

Balloon Books. *What Do You Say?* 2002.

Ishida, Jui (Illustrator) & Random, Melanie (Designer). *Who Says Baa?: A Touch and Feel Board Book.* Piggy Toes Press, 2003.

Miller, Margaret. *Baby Pets*. Little Simon, 2003.

St. Martin's Press. *Animals*. 2004.

Stanley, Mandy. *On the Farm*. Kingfisher, 2002.

Swine, Ima & Meredith, Shelley (Illustrator). *How to Be a Pig*. Price Stern Sloan, 2002.

Vine, Bo & Meredith, Shelley (Illustrator). *How to Be a Cow*. Price Stern Sloan, 2002.

Ziefert, Harriet & Taback, Simms. *Noisy Barn!* Blue Apple Books, 2003.

ANIMALS—EXOTIC

Burnard, Damon & Cairns, Julia (Illustrator). *I Spy in the Jungle*. Chronicle Books, 2001.

Burnard, Damon & Cairns, Julia (Illustrator). *I Spy in the Ocean*. Chronicle Books, 2001.

McCurry, Kristen & Jackson, Aimee. *Desert Babies*. NorthWord Press, 2003.

Pingry, Patricia A., Sharp, Chris (Illustrator) & San Diego Zoo (Photographer). *Baby Zebra*. CandyCane Press, 2004.

ANIMALS—FICTION

Anderson, Airlie. *A Very Furry Flap Book*. Tiger Tales, 2004.

Anderson, Airlie. *A Very Flap Book*. Tiger Tales, 2004.

Anderson, Airlie. *A Very Spotty flap Book*. Tiger Tales, 2004.

Anderson, Airlie. *A Very Stripy flap Book*. Tiger Tales, 2004.

Boynton, Sandra. *Fuzzy, Fuzzy, Fuzzy!: A Touch, Skritch, & Tickle Book*. Little Simon, 2003.

Carle, Eric. *Does a Kangaroo Have a Mother, Too?* HarperFestival, 2002.

Engelbreit, Mary. *Booky*. Harper Festival, 2003.

Fox, Christyan & Fox, Diane. *What's the Opposite, PiggyWiggy?* Handprint Books, 2002.

Jareckie, Ellen. *A Mouse in the House*. Little, Brown, 2003.

Lionni, Leo. *Let's Make Rabbits*. Alfred A. Knopf, 2002.

Mastrangelo, Judy. *What Do Bunnies Do All Day?* CandyCane Press, 2003.

McMullan, Kate & Lemaître, Pascal. *Supercat*. Workman Publishing, 2002.

Murphy, Mary. *I Kissed the Baby!* Candlewick Press, 2005.

Porter-Gaylord, Laurel & Wolff, Ashley (Illustrator). *I Love My Daddy Because—*. Dutton Children's Books, 2004.

Porter-Gaylord, Laurel & Wolff, Ashley (Illustrator). *I Love My Mommy Because—*. Dutton Children's Books, 2004.

Powell, Alma. *My Little Wagon*. HarperFestival, 2003.

Quinlan, Heather. *Silly Dog*. Sterling Publishing Company, 2003.

Root, Phyllis & Meade, Holly (Illustrator). *Hop!* Candlewick Press, 2005.

Root, Phyllis & Meade, Holly (Illustrator). *Quack!* Candlewick Press, 2005.

Ross, David & Rader, Laura (Illustrator). *A Book of Hugs*. HarperCollins/HarperFestival, 2002.

Ross, David & Rader, Laura (Illustrator). *A Book of Kisses*. HarperCollins/HarperFestival, 2002.

Rowe, Jeannette. *Yoyo's Animal Friends*. Tiger Tales, 2002.

Schindel, John & Marigo, Luiz Claudio. *Busy Monkeys*. Tricycle Press, 2002.

Simmons, Jane. *Daisy says, Here We Go Round the Mulberry Bush*. Little, Brown, 2002.

Sterling. *Sleepy Cat*. 2003.

Sterling. *Sleepy Dog*. 2003.

Walters, Catherine. *Are You There, Baby Bear?* Dutton Children's Books, 2003.

Walton, Rick & Miglio, Paige (Illustrator). *So Many Bunnies: a Bedtime ABC and Counting Book*. HarperFestival, 2000.

Watt, Fiona & Wells, Rachel (Illustrator). *Dinosaurs*. Usborne Publishing, 2005.

Wildsmith, Brian. *Brian Wildsmith's Zoo Animals*. Star Bright Books, 2002.

Yoon, Salina. *My Puppy*. Price Stern Sloan, 2004.

Ziefert, Harriet & Cohen, Santiago (Illustrator). *Kitty Says Meow*. Grosset & Dunlap, 2002.

Ziefert, Harriet & Taback, Simms. *Zoo Parade!* Blue Apple Books, 2003.

BEDTIME/BATHTIME

Collins, Terry & Ellis, Art (Illustrator). *Bob's Bedtime*. Simon Spotlight, 2003.

Cratzius, Barbara & Thonissen, Ute (Illustrator). *Good Night, Sleep Tight!* Parklane Publishing, 2004.

Ellis, Libby. *Bubble Bath Baby*. Chronicle Books, 2004.

Hest, Amy & Jeram, Anita (Illustrator). *Kiss Good Night*. Candlewick Press, 2004.

Lee, Quinlan B. & Johnson, Jay B (Illustrator). *Sweet Dreams!* Scholastic, 2005.

Lucchesi, E. & Brannon, Tom (Illustrator). *Bear Loves Bedtime!* Simon Spotlight, 2003.

King, Sue. *Time for Bed*. Chronicle Books, 2004.

Smee, Nicola. *Splish! Splash!* Barron's Educational Series, 2002.

Sykes, Julie & Warnes, Tom (Illustrator). *Bathtime, Little Tiger!* Tiger Tales, 2003.

Wolski, Peter, Brunhoff, Laurent de (Character Creator), & Brunhoff, Jean de (Character Creator). *Babar Bedtime*. Harry N. Abrams, 2004.

COLORS

DK Publishing, Inc. *Rainbow Colors*. 2004.

Fremont, Eleanor & Schigiel, Gregg (Illustrator). *Colors with Oswald*. Simon Spotlight/Nick Jr., 2004.

Niehaus, Alisha., Brannon, Tom (Art Adaptor)., & Schulz, Charles M. *Colors*. Little Simon, 2004.

Parett, Lisa. *Princess Colors*. Sterling Publishing Company, 2004.

Rowe, Jeannette. *Yoyo's Colors*. Tiger Tales, 2002.

Twinem, Neecy. *Baby Gecko's Colors*. Rising Moon, 2004.

ETTIQUETTE

De Beer, Hans. *Lars Helps Out.* Sterling Publishing Company, 2003.

Hallinan, P. K. *Let's Be Helpful.* CandyCane Press, 2004.

Hallinan, P. K. *Let's Be Honest.* CandyCane Press, 2003

Hallinan, P. K. *Let's Be Kind.* CandyCane Press, 2003

Hallinan, P. K. *Let's Be Polite.* CandyCane Press, 2004

Hallinan, P. K. *Let's Play as a Team.* 2002.

Hallinan, P. K. *Let's Share.* 2002.

FAMILY

Benkowski, Paul Vos & Herbert, Jennifer (Illustrator). *Mama's Home!* Chronicle Books, 2004.

Cousins, Lucy. *Maisy Loves You.* Candlewick Press, 2003.

Ellis, Libby. *Birthday Baby.* Chronicle Books, 2004.

Ellwand, David (Photographer). *I Love You!* Silver Dolphin Books, 2004.

Engelbreit, Mary. *Lovey Dovey.* Harper Festival, 2003.

Gentieu, Penny. *Grow! Babies!* Crown Publishers, 2002.

Kassirer, Sue & Smith, Jerry (Illustrator). *What Daddy Loves.* Reader's Digest Children's Books, 2003.

Katz, Karen. *Daddy and Me.* Simon & Schuster Children's Publishing, 2003.

Katz, Karen. *Grandma and Me: A Lift-the-Flap Book.* Little Simon, 2002.

Katz, Karen. *Grandpa and Me: A Lift-the-Flap Book.* Little Simon, 2004.

Katz, Karen. *Where Is Baby's Mommy?: A Lift-the-Flap Book.* Little Simon/Simon & Schuster Books for Children, 2000.

Kubler, Annie. *Waiting for Baby.* Child's Play (International) Ltd., 2000.

Lagonegro, Melissa. *A Touch of Love: With Art from the Morehead Collection.* Random House, 2004.

Lewis, Rose A. & Dyer, Jane (Illustrator). *I Love You like Crazy Cakes*. Little, Brown, 2002.

Maccarone, Grace & Williams, Sam. *Bless Me*. Scholastic, 2004.

McCourt, Lisa & Moore, Cyd (Illustrator). *I LoveYou, Stinky Face*. Scholastic, 2004.

Merritt, Kate. *My Mom: With Flaps to Open*. Sterling Publishing, 2002.

Merritt, Kate. *My Sister: With Flaps to Open*. Sterling Publishing, 2003.

Meyers, Susan & Frazee, Marla (Illustrator). *Everywhere Babies*. Red Wagon Books, 2004.

Newman, Marjorie & Benson, Patrick (Illustrator). *Mole and the Baby Bird*. Bloomsbury Children's Books, 2004.

Page, Josephine & Morgan, Mary. *Mommy Loves Her Bunny*. Scholastic, 2003.

Pandell, Karen & Cowen-Fletcher, Jane (Illustrator). *I Love You Baby from Head to Toe!* Candlewick Press, 2004.

Priddy Books. *Our New Baby*, 2004.

Rossetti-Shustak, Bernadette & Church, Caroline Jayne (Illustrator). *I Love You Through and Through*. Scholastic, Inc., 2005.

Scott, Michael. *Skidamarink! I Love You*. Hyperion Books for Children, 2004.

Shannon, David. *Oops!* Blue Sky Press, 2005.

Shannon, David. *Oh, David!* Blue Sky Press, 2005.

Silver Dolphin Books. *Baby's Day!* 2004.

Simpson, Valerie, Ashford, Nickolas, & Smith, Charles R., Jr. (Photographer). *Ain't No Mountain High Enough*. Jump at the Sun/Hyperion Books for Children, 2002.

Stephens, Monique Z. & Yee, Josie (Illustrator). *Apple Dumplin's Day*. Grosset & Dunlap, 2003.

Tafuri, Nancy. *You Are Special, Little One*. Scholastic Press, 2004.

Uff, Caroline. *Hello, Lulu*. Walker & Co., 2004.

Wilson, Sarah & Sweet, Melissa (Illustrator). *Love and Kisses*. Candlewick Press, 2002.

FOOD

Baicker, Karen & Williams, Sam (Illustrator). *Yum Tummy Tickly!* Handprint Books, 2004.

Patricelli, Leslie. *Yummy, YUCKY.* Candlewick Press, 2003.

Sanger, Amy Wilson. *A Little Bit of Soul Food.* Tricycle Press, 2004.

Sanger, Amy Wilson. *Yum Yum Dim Sum.* Tricycle Press, 2003.

Zoehfeld, Kathleen Weidner & Santoro, Christopher (Illustrator). *Apples, Apples.* HarperFestival, 2004.

HISTORY/PATRIOTIC/UNITED STATES

Bellamy, Francis. *I Pledge Allegiance—.* Star Spangled Baby, 2003.

DK Publishing, Inc. *Washington, D.C. Board Book.* 2004.

Ellis, Libby. *Buckaroo Baby.* Chronicle Books, 2004.

Epstein, Brad M. (Editor). *Yale University 101: My First Text-Board-Book.* Michaelson Entertainment, 2003.

Mead, David & Sharp, Chris (Pictures). *A Little Abraham Lincoln Learns to Be Honest.* Virtue Books, 2003.

Random, Lily & Berg, Michelle (Illustrator). *Celebrate America.* Price, Stern, Sloan, 2003.

MISCELLANEOUS

DK Publishing. *My First Body Board Book.* 2004.

Knudsen, Michelle & Thornburgh, Bethann (Illustrator). *Princess Party.* Little Simon, 2003.

Scarry, Richard. *Richard Scarry's Goldbug & Co.* Golden Books, 2004.

Weeks, Sarah & Kaminsky, Jef (Pictures). *Bite Me, I'm a Book.* Random House, 2002.

Zagarenski, Pamela. *What Am I Playing?* Houghton Mifflin Company, 2004.

MOVEABLE/TEXTURED BOOKS

Blakeslee, Ann R. & Palma, Anna (Photographer). *Go, Baby, Go!* Scholastic, 2005.

Blakeslee, Ann R. & Palma, Anna (Photographer). *Play, Baby, Play!* Scholastic, 2005.

Courtin, Thierry. *Let's Play, Baby.* Sterling, 2002.

DK Publishing. *Ready, Set, Go!* 2004.

DK Publishing. *Quack, Quack!* 2004.

Gerstein, Sherry & Van Fleet, Mara (Illustrator). *My Great Aunt Philbian.* Reader's Digest Children's Books, 2004.

Jones, Lara. *Fun on the Beach.* Barron's, 2002.

Jones, Lara. *Fun on the Farm.* Barron's, 2002.

Jones, Lara. *Fun at the Zoo.* Barron's, 2002.

Nickelson, Jessica & Novak, Matthew (Illustrator). *Five Little Monsters: Glow-in-the-Dark Boogly Eyes!* Little Simon, 2003.

Price Stern Sloan. *Teddy Bear, Teddy Bear, Touch Your Nose.* 2000.

Random, Melanie (Designer) & Ishida, Jui (Illustrator). *Who Says Moo?: A Touch and Feel Board Book.* Piggy Toes Press, 2003.

Savary, Fabien (Text & Concept Writer), Vadeboncoeur, Isabelle (Text & Concept Writer), Depratto, Marcel (Coloration), Dupras, Monique (Artistic Director), & Tipeo (Illustrator). *Caillou: What's Inside?* Chouette Publishing, 2002.

Shulman, Mark & Harris, Jenny B. (Illustrator). *Super Sports.* Sterling Publishing Company, 2003.

Shulman, Mark & Harris, Jenny B. (Illustrator). *Amazing Animals.* Sterling Publishing Company, 2003.

Silver Dolphin Books. *Squeak, Squeak!* 2004.

Silverhardt, Lauryn, Greenblatt, C.H. (Illustrator), & Reiss, William (Illustrator). *SpongeBob's Best Day Ever!* Simon Spotlight/Nickelodeon, 2004.

Sirett, Dawn. *At Home.* DK Publishing, 2002.

Tripathi, Namtata., Norris, Ami., & Couri, Kathy (Illustrator). *Happy Graduation.* HarperFestival, 2003.

Watt, Fiona & Wells, Rachel (Illustrator). *That's Not My Car.* EDC Publishing, 2004.

Watt, Fiona & Wells, Rachel (Illustrator). *That's Not My Dinosaur.* EDC Publishing, 2002.

Watt, Fiona & Wells, Rachel (Illustrator). *That's Not My Kitten*. EDC Publishing, 2001.

Watt, Fiona & Wells, Rachel (Illustrator). *That's Not My Monster.* EDC Publishing, 2004.

Watt, Fiona & Wells, Rachel (Illustrator). *That's Not My Puppy*. EDC Publishing, 2000.

MUSIC/ART

Raschka, Christopher. *Charlie Parker Played Be Bop*. Orchard Books, 2004.

Merberg, Julie & Bober, Suzanne. *A Picnic with Monet*. Chronicle Books, 2003.

Merberg, Julie & Bober, Suzanne. *Dancing with Degas*. Chronicle Books, 2003.

Merberg, Julie & Bober, Suzanne. *In the Garden with Van Gogh*. Chronicle Books, 2002.

Salmansohn, Karen & Stauffer, Brian (Illustrator). *Art*. Tricycle, 2003.

NATURE/TRIPS/OUTDOORS

Allen, Francesca (Designer & Illustrator), Litchfield, Jo (Modelmaker), & Allman, Howard (Photographer). *Beach*. EDC Publishing, 2004.

Barron's Educational Series, Inc. *On the Water: Five Fun Characters with Five Fun Rhymes*. 2003.

Stanley, Mandy. *In the Park*. Kingfisher, 2004.

Stanley, Mandy. *At the Pool*. Kingfisher, 2004.

Schimmel, Schim. *Children of the Earth Remembered*. Northword, 2002.

Schimmel, Schim. *The Family of Earth*. Northword, 2002.

NUMBERS/COUNTING

Henson, Jim (Character Creator) & Pantuso, Mike (Illustrator). *1, 2, 3 by Elmo*. Random House, 2001.

Hoffman, Don & Dakins, Todd (Illustrator). *A Counting Book: With Billy & Abigail*. Dalmatian Press, 2004.

Pfister, Marcus. *Rainbow Fish Counting*. North-South Books, 2004.

Rowe, Jeannette. *Yoyo's Numbers*. Tiger Tales, 2002.

Saint-Exupéry, Antoine de. *Counting with the Little Prince*. Harcourt, 2003.

Scott, Michael (Photographer). *Five Little Pumpkins*. Hyperion Books for Children, 2003.

Schulman, Janet & So, Meilo (Illustrator). *Countdown to Spring: An Animal Counting Book*. Alfred A. Knopf, 2004.

Twinem, Neecy. *Baby Coyote Counts*. Rising Moon, 2004.

NURSERY RHYMES & OTHER RHYMING BOOKS

Cohen, Santiago. *Fiddle-I-Fee*. Blue Apple Books, 2003.

Kemp, Moira. *Round and Round the Garden*. McGraw Hill Children's Publishing, 2003.

Mavor, Salley. *Hey, Diddle, Diddle!* Houghton Mifflin, 2005.

Mavor, Salley. *Mary Had a Little Lamb*, Houghton Mifflin, 2005.

Opie, Iona (Compiler) & Wells, Rosemary (Illustrator). *Wee Willie Winkie and Other Rhymes*. Candlewick Press, 2001.

Pearson, Tracey Campbell. *Diddle, Diddle Dumpling*. Farrar Straus & Giroux, 2005.

Pearson, Tracey Campbell. *Little Bo Peep*. Farrar Straus & Giroux, 2004.

Pearson, Tracey Campbell. *Little Miss Muffet*. Farrar Straus & Giroux, 2005.

Smith, Jessie Willcox & Nudelman, Edward D. (Editor). *Mother Goose for Kids*. Pelican Pub. Company, 2004.

Westcott, Nadine Bernard. *I Know an Old Lady Who Swallowed a Fly*. Little, Brown, 2003.

SEASONS/WEATHER

Burg, Ann & Asbury, Kelly (Illustrator). *Winter Walk*. Harper Festival, 2003.

Cousins, Lucy. *Maisy's Seasons*. Candlewick Press, 2002.

DK Publishing. *Four Seasons*. 2004.

DK Publishing. *Weather.* 2003.

Shoolbred, Catherine & Pichon, Liz (Illustrator). *Friendly Snowman.* Candlewick Press, 2003.

SHAPES & SIZES

DK Publishing. *Shapes.* 2002.

Hays, Anna Jane & Moroney, Christopher (Illustrator). *So Big!* Random House, 2003.

Parr, Todd. *Big & Little.* Little, Brown, 2001.

Silverhardt, Lauryn & Giarrano, Vince (Illustrator). *Let's Find Shapes.* Simon Spotlight, 2002.

Tripathi, Namrata & Murawski, Kevin (Illustrator). *Big, Bigger, Biggest!* HarperFestival, 2005.

SPANISH

Ellis, Liby. *Buenos Dias Baby.* Chronicle Books, 2004.

Christelow, Eileen. *Cinco Monitos brincando en la Cama [Five Little Monkeys Jumping on the Bed].* Clarion Books, 2005.

Emberley, Rebecca. *My Numbers [Mis Numeros].* Little, Brown and Company, 2000.

Magoon, Scott. *Peek-a-Boo Family.* Berlitz, 2005.

Zagarenski, Pamela. *What Day Is It [Qué día es]?* Houghton Mifflin Company, 2005.

TRANSPORTATION

Awdry, W. & Red Giraffe (Illustrator). *Thomas & Friends on the Track [Thomas & Friends There and Back].* Random House, 2004.

Bryant, Ray. *Up in the Sky: Five Fun Characters with Five Fun Rhymes.* Barron's Educational Series, 2003.

Carey, Craig Robert & Artful Doodlers (Illustrator). *The Steamroller.* Scholastic, 2004.

Gergely, Tibor. *The Fire Engine Book.* Golden Books, 2004.

Hart, Simon. *Go, Go, Trucks!* Price Stern Sloan, 2004.

Hart, Simon. *Go, Go, Planes!* Price Stern Sloan, 2004.

Litchfield, Jo (Designer & Modelmaker). *Trucks*. Usborne, 2002.

Mayer, Mercer. *Just a Dump Truck*. HarperCollins, 2005.

Rindone, Nancy L. & SI Artists (Illustrator). *Cars, Trucks, Planes, and Trains*. Reader's Digest Children's Books, 2004.

St. Martin's Press. *Trucks*, 2004.

To learn more about literacy and language development and strategies for promoting it, consider reading:

Linebarger, D. (2004). Young children, language, and television. *LITERACY Today, 40,* 20–21.

Moss, G., Swim, T. J., Cross, D. J., Sholl, P., & Laidroo, I. (2005). *Annual Editions: Early Childhood and Elementary Literacy 05/06.* Dubuque, IA: McGraw-Hill/Dushkin,

NAEYC (1995). Responding to linguistic and cultural diversity: Recommendations for effective early childhood education. Available at http://www.naeyc.org. On the home page, do a search for Positions and then click on Position Statements.

Rosenquest, B. B. (2002). Literacy-based planning and pedagogy that supports toddler language development. *Early Childhood Education Journal, 29,* 241–249.

Zeece, P. D., & Churchill, S. L. (2001). First stories: Emergent literacy in infants and toddlers. *Early Childhood Education Journal, 29,* 101–104.

In addition, NAEYC has compiled lists of children's books on particular subjects that are available online through *Beyond the Journal*. To illustrate, you can find such a list about health and safety and other topics at http://www.journal.naeyc.org. On the home page, do a search for Children's Books.

PROFESSIONAL ORGANIZATIONS

When looking to further your development, a professional organization is a great place to start. There are several organizations, some of which have state or local affiliates.

National Association for the Education of Young Children (NAEYC)
1509 16th Street, NW
Washington, DC 20036
800-424-2460
http://www.naeyc.org
E-mail membership@naeyc.org

Specific membership benefits:
Comprehensive Members receive all the benefits of Regular membership plus annually receive five or six books immediately after their release by NAEYC.

Regular and Student Members benefits:

- Six issues of *Young Children*, which includes timely articles on pertinent issues, as well as suggestions and strategies for enhancing children's learning
- Access to *Beyond the Journal,* which is a Web-based component of the journal that contains additional articles, resource lists, and other documents that are not included in the print issue
- Reduced registration fees at NAEYC-sponsored local and national conferences and seminars
- Discounted prices on hundreds of books, videos, brochures, and posters from NAEYC's extensive catalog of materials

- Access to the *Members Only* Web site, including links to additional resources and chat sites for communication with other professionals

National Association of Child Care Professionals (NACCP)
P.O. Box 90723
Austin, TX 78709
800-537-1118
http://www.naccp.org

Specific membership benefits:

Management Tools of the Trade™
Your membership provides complete and FREE access (a $79 value) to these effective management tools that provide technical assistance in human resource management. In addition, as a member, you will receive NACCP's quarterly trade journals, *Professional Connections©*, *Teamwork©*, and *Caring for Your Children©*, to help you stay on top of hot issues in child care. Each edition also includes a Tool of the Trade™.

National Child Care Association (NCCA)
1016 Rosser St.
Conyers, GA 30012
800-543-7161
http://www.nccanet.org

Specific membership benefits:
As the only recognized voice in Washington D.C., NCCA has great influence on our legislators. Professional development opportunities are also available.

Association for Education International (ACEI)
The Olney Professional Building
17904 Georgia Avenue, Suite 215
Olney, MD 20832
800-423-2563 or 301-570-2122
301-570-2212 (fax)
http://www.acei.org

ACEI is an international organization dedicated to promoting the best educational practices throughout the world.

Specific membership benefits:
- Workshops and travel/study tours abroad

- Four issues per year of the *Childhood Education* journal and the *Journal of Research in Childhood Education*
- Hundreds of resources for parents and teachers, including books, pamphlets, audiotapes, and videotapes

National AfterSchool Association (NAA)
1137 Washington Street
Boston, MA 02124
617-298-5012
617-298-5022 (fax)
http://www.naaweb.org

NAA is a national organization dedicated to providing information, technical assistance, and resources concerning children in out-of-school programs. Members include teachers, policy makers, and administrators representing all public, private, and community-based sectors of after-school programs.

Specific member benefits:
- A subscription to the NAA journal, *School-Age Review*
- A companion membership in state affiliates
- Discounts on NAA publications and products
- Discount on NAA annual conference registration
- Opportunity to be an NAA accreditation endorser
- Public policy representatives in Washington, D.C.

OTHER ORGANIZATIONS TO CONTACT

The American Academy of Child and Adolescent Psychiatry
3615 Wisconsin Ave., NW
Washington, DC 20016-3007
202-966-7300
202-966-2891 (fax)
http://www.aacap.org/

Baby Watch for Early Intervention
PO Box 144720
Salt Lake City, UT 84114-4720
800-961-4226
http://www.utahbabywatch.org/

California First 5
California Children & Families Commission
501 J Street, Suite 530

Sacramento, CA 95814
916-323-0056
916-323-0069 (fax)
http://www.ccfc.ca.gov/

Child Care Aware
1319 F Street, NW
Suite 500
Washington, DC 20004
800-424-2246
202-787-5116 (fax)
http://www.childcareaware.org/

Children's Advocate
Action Alliance for Children
1201 Martin Luther King Jr. Way
Oakland, CA 94612
510-444-7136
http://www.4children.org/

The Children's Defense Fund
25 E. St. NW
Washington, DC 20001
202-628-8787
http://www.childrensdefense.org

CITE—Coalition of Infant/Toddler Educators
PO Box 141
Monmouth Junction, NJ 08852
201-996-2987
http://www.njcite.org/
Connect for Kids
1625 K St., NW (11th floor)
Washington, DC 20006
http://www.connectforkids.org/

National Association for Family Child Care
P.O. Box 10373
Des Moines, IA 50306
800-359-3817
http://www.nafcc.org
Journal: *The National Perspective*

National Black Child Development Institute
1023 15th Ave. NW
Washington, DC 20002

202-833-2220
http://www.nbcdi.org

National Child Care Information Center
10530 Rosehaven St.
Suite 400
Fairfax, VA 22030
800-616-2242
800-716-2242 (fax)
http://www.nccic.org/

National Head Start Association
1651 Prince Street
Alexandria, VA 22314
703-739-0875
http://www.nhsa.org
Journal: *Children and Families*

International Society for the Prevention of Child Abuse and Neglect
25 W. 560 Geneva Road
Suite L2C
Carol Stream, IL 60188
630-221-1311
http://www.ipscan.org

Journal: *Child Abuse and Neglect: The International Journal*
Council for Exceptional Children
1110N. Glebe Road
Suite 300
Arlington, VA 22201
888-CEC-SPED
http://www.cec.sped.org
Journal: *CEC Today*

National Association for Bilingual Education
Union Center Plaza
810 First Street, NE
Washington, DC 20002
http://www.nabe.org
Journal: *NABE Journal of Research and Practice*

International Reading Association
800 Barksdale Road
P.O. Box 8139
Newark, DE 19714
800-336-READ

http://www.reading.org
Journal: *The Reading Teacher*

National Education Organization (NEA)
1201 16th St. NW
Washington, DC 20036
202-833-4000
http://www.nea.org
Journals: *Works4Me* and *NEA Focus*, by online subscription

PITC: The Program for Infant/Toddler Caregivers
WestEd PITC
180 Harbor Drive
Suite 112
Sausalito, CA 94965-1410
415-289-2300
415-289-2301 (fax)
http://www.pitc.org/

WestEd
730 Harrison Street
San Francisco, CA 94107
877-4-WestEd
415-565-3000
415-565-3012 (fax)
http://www.wested.org/

World Association for Infant Mental Health
Hiram E. Fitzgerald, Executive Director
University Outreach & Engagement
Kellogg Center, Garden Level, #24
Michigan State University
East Lansing, MI USA 48824
517-432-3793
517-432-3694 (fax)
http://www.waimh.org/

Zero to Three: National Center for Infants, Toddlers, and Families
2000M. Street NW
Suite 200
Washington, DC 20036
202-638-1144
http://www.zerotothree.org
Journal: *Zero to Three*

ADDITIONAL RESOURCES

Articles for further reading were provided at the end of each section throughout this book. This list provides additional resources that may assist you in your professional development.

BOOKS

Aronson, S. S. (Ed.), & complied with P. M. Spahr. (2002). *Healthy young children: A manual for programs.* Washington, DC: NAEYC.

Baker, A. C., & Manfredi/Petitt, L. A. (2004). *Relationships, the heart of quality care: Creating community among adults in early care settings.* Washington, DC: NAEYC.

Bergen, D., Reid, R., & Torelli, L. (2001). *Educating and caring for very young children: The infant/toddler curriculum.* New York: Teachers College Press.

Cassidy, J., & Shaver, P.R. (Eds.). (1999). *Handbook of attachment: Theory, research, and clinical application.* New York: Guilford Press.

Curtis, D., & Cater, M. (2000). *The art of awareness: How observation can transform your teaching.* St. Paul, MN: Redleaf Press.

Gandini, L., & Edwards, C. P. (Eds.). (2001). *Bambini: The Italian approach to infant/toddler care.* New York: Teachers College Press.

Gronlund, G. (2003). *Focused early learning: A planning framework for teaching young children.* St. Paul, MN: Redleaf Press.

Grossmann, K.E., Grossmann, K., & Waters, E. (Eds.). (2005). *Attachment from infants to adulthood: The major longitudinal studies.* New York: Guilford Press.

Helm, J. H., Beneke, S., & Steinheimer, K. (1998). *Windows on learning: Documenting young children's work.* New York: Teachers College Press.

Herr, J., & Swim, T. (2003). *Birth to 6 months: Rattle time, face to face, and many other activities for infants: Creative resources for infant and toddler series.* Clifton Park, NY: Thomson Delmar Learning.

Herr, J., & Swim, T. (2003). *7 to 12 months: Making sounds, making music, and many other activities for infants: Creative resources for infant and toddler series.* Clifton Park, NY: Thomson Delmar Learning.

Herr, J., & Swim, T. (2003). *13 to 24 months: Sorting shapes, show me, and many other activities for toddlers: Creative resources for infant and toddler series.* Clifton Park, NY: Thomson Delmar Learning.

Herr, J., & Swim, T. (2003). *25 to36 months: Rhyming books, marble painting, and many other activities for toddlers: Creative resources for infant and toddler series.* Clifton Park, NY: Thomson Delmar Learning.

Herr, J., & Swim, T. (2002). *Creative resources for infants and toddlers.* (2nd ed.). Cliffton Park, NY: Thomson Delmar Learning.

Honig, A. (2002). Secure relationships: *Nurturing infant/toddler attachment in early care settings.* Washington, DC: NAEYC.

Hyson, M. (2004). *The emotional development of young children: Building an emotion-centered curriculum.* (2nd ed.). New York: Teachers College Press.

Jablon, J. R., Dombro, A. L., & Dichtelmiller, M. L. (1999). *The power of observation.* Washington, DC: Teaching Strategies.

Lombardi, J. (2003). *Time to care: Redesigning child care to promote education, support families, and build communities.* Philadelphia, PA: Temple University Press.

Marion, M. (2004). *Using observation in early childhood education.* Upper Saddle River, NJ: Pearson Merrill Prentice Hall.

Osofsky, J., & Fitzgerald, H. E. (Eds.). (2000). *Handbook of infant mental health.* New York: Wiley.

Petrie, S., & Owens, S. (Eds.). (2005). *Authentic relationships in group care of infants and toddlers: Resources for infant educarers (RIE) principles into practice.* London, England: J. Kingsley Publishers.

Project Zero and Reggio Children. (2001). *Making learning visible: Children as individual and group learners.* Reggio Emilia, Italy: Reggio Children srl.

Raines, S., Miller, K., & Curry-Rood, L. (2002). *Story s-t-r-e-t-c-h-e-r-s for infants, toddlers and twos: Experiences, activities, and games for popular children's books.* Beltsville, MD: Gryphon House.

Zigler, E. (2002). *The first three years and beyond: Brain development and social policy.* New Haven, CT: Yale University Press.

INTERNET RESOURCES

CEED—Center for Early Education and Development
University of Minnesota
Pattee Hall, 150 Pillsbury Drive SE
Minneapolis, MN 55455
612-624-5780
612-625-2093 (fax)
http://education.umn.edu. On the home page, do a search for CEED.

Earlychildhood NEWS
2 Lower Ragsdale Drive
Suite 200
Monterey, CA 93940
831-333-5505
831-333-5510 (fax)
http://www.earlychildhood.com/

Education Week & Teacher Magazine
Editorial Projects in Education Inc.
Suite 100
6935 Arlington Road
Bethesda, MD 20814-5233
800-346-1834
301-280-3100
Education Week: (301) 280-3200 (fax)
Teacher Magazine: (301) 280-3150 (fax)
http://www.edweek.org/

ERIC Project
Computer Sciences Corporation
4483-A Forbes Blvd.
Lanham, MD 20706
800-LET-ERIC (800-538-3742)
http://www.eric.ed.gov/

National Center for Early Development and Learning
FPG Child Development Institute
CB 8185
Chapel Hill, NC 27599-8185
919-966-7180
http://www.fpg.unc.edu/

Journals related to infants and toddlers:

Infant & Child Development
John Wiley & Sons, Inc.
Attn: Journals Admin Dept UK
111 River Street
Hoboken, NJ 07030
201-748-6645

Infant Mental Health Journal
John Wiley & Sons, Inc.
Attn: Journals Admin Dept UK
111 River Street
Hoboken, NJ 07030
201-748-6645

Infants & Young Children: An Interdisciplinary Journal of Special Care Practices
Lippincott Williams & Wilkins
351 West Camden Street
Baltimore, MD 21201
http://www.iycjournal.com/

ADDITIONAL PROFESSIONAL RESOURCES

Infant Social and Emotional Health
Children's Mental Health Initiative
University of Washington
Maternal and Child Health Program
Box 357230
Seattle, WA 98195-7230
206-543-8819
206-616-8370 (fax)
http://www.washington.edu/. On the home page, do a search for Maternal and Child Health Program.

National Early Childhood Technical Assistance Center
Campus Box 8040, UNC-CH

Chapel Hill, NC 27599-8040
919-962-2001
919-966-7463 (fax)
http://www.nectac.org/

National Network for Child Care
Iowa State University Extension
1094 LeBaron Hall
Ames, IA 50001
http://www.nncc.org/

VIDEOS FOR CAREGIVERS

- *Getting "in tune:" Creating nurturing relationships with infants and toddlers.* (1988). Produced and directed by Butterfield, G. Joint project of WestEd and California Department of Education, Sacramento, CA: California Department of Education. Information about PITC program and videos is available at http://www.wested.org.

- *For the love of Julian.* (1999). Produced by Balustein, M., & Kasell, D. New York: WinStar Cinema.

- *Inclusive child care for infants and toddlers: Meeting individual and special needs.* (1997). Baltimore, MD: Brooks Publishing.

- *The Next step: Including the infant in the curriculum.* (2001). Lally, J. R., et al. Program for Infant/Toddler Caregivers (PITC). Joint project of WestEd and California Department of Education, Sacramento, CA: California Department of Education. Information available on PITC program and videos at http://www.wested.org

- *Nurturing.* San Luis Obispo, CA: Davidson Films. Information about videos can be found at http://www.davidsonfilms.com or by calling toll free 1-888-437-4200. The company also has a cluster of Early Childhood films that are very informative. Many are designed for preschool teachers but provide solid information about early development and learning.

- *Young children in action.* (2000). Produced by Bergen, D., Reid, R., & Torelli, L. Oxford, OH: Miami University. Film is distributed by Teachers College Press, 1234 Amsterdam Ave., New York, NY 10027.

ISSUES AND TRENDS

Many issues face new teachers. The goal of this book has been to assist you with becoming a professional infant and toddler educator by highlighting some of these issues and providing the opportunity for you to reflect on them by reading articles and responding to questions and case studies. If you have completed the book to this point, then you are aware of many issues facing infant and toddler teachers—for example, infant brain development, continuity of care, family-style grouping, developmentally appropriate practices, and individualized curriculum. The issues of brain development, continuity of care, and family-style grouping are connected, as they serve to address the interrelatedness of the developmental aspects of attachment, security, and growth of relationships for infants and toddlers and their families. Suggestions in the articles included earlier support you in applying your knowledge of development to your work with very young children.

Another concern for infant and toddler teachers involves protecting and promoting the children's health and safety. Although this issue has not been addressed so far in this book, it is no less important for teachers to understand. One of your foundational guides about health and safety will be your state's child care regulations. Most states clearly outline their expectations for protecting the welfare of the children in your care. Often, beginning teachers feel overwhelmed by the number of regulations that they must remember and consider in their daily work. However, there are many strategies for assisting in this area. For example, if the cribs must be a certain number of inches apart, then arrange them as you desire, measure, and mark the flooring with tape. This way, you can quickly check the spacing of the cribs, know that you are in compliance with the state regulations, and not have to worry further. Moreover, copying relevant guidelines and posting them on the insides of cupboard doors can help to refresh your memory of important regulations. As you may know, state regulations are considered minimal standards, so you should consider moving beyond them to NAEYC's accreditation standards. These newly revised and approved standards, which are now divided by age, are available on the organization's Web site at: http://www.naeyc.org. Click on Accreditation, and then click on New Standards and Criteria.

Infant and toddler teachers can no longer just be mindful of protecting the safety of children. More and more children come to child care programs with serious health concerns. It is our ethical responsibility to partner with families to promote the optimal well-being of children. This means that you must be "armed" with information. A recently compiled and thorough list of resources about health and safety found at http://www.journal.naeyc.org can assist with this task. On the home page, search for the Health and Safety Resources links.